THE LAST PHASE OF LIFE

THE LAST PHASE OF LIFE IS AN INSPIRATIONAL BOOK WRITTEN BY ASHFAQ AHMED

ASHFAQ AHMED

The LAST PHASE OF LIFE

A LITTLE WORLD WITHOUT HOPE

COLLECTION OF SHORT STORIES ON LIFE

(ASHFAQ AHMED)

Contents

Contents

Foreword

ASHFAQ AHMED

ABOUT THE AUTHOR

Ashfaq Ahmed is a name among million who struggled, Failed and surged ahead in the search of success, happiness and contentiment. Just like any middle class guy, he too had a bunch of unclear dreams and blurred vision of his goals in life. All he had was an undying learning attitude to hold on to. Rowing through ups and downs, it was time that taught him the real meaning of life. Recently I published a book the last phase of life this is my second book in which I talk about the hope.

About the book

"LAST PHASE OF LIFEUnlocking Purpose, Passion, and Progress" is a transformative book that delves into the profound impact of understanding THE POWER OF HOPE in life. It explores the importance of having a clear sense of purpose and how it can fuel our motivation, guide our decisions, and lead to a more fulfilling and meaningful existence.

Written by renowned author (Ashfaq Ahmed) the book combines personal anecdotes,

scientific research, and practical exercises to help readers uncover their unique purpose and align their actions with their deepest values and desires. It offers a roadmap for discovering one's passions, overcoming obstacles, and achieving personal and professional growth.

Throughout the pages, readers will embark on a journey of self-reflection, questioning their assumptions, beliefs, and goals. The book emphasizes the significance of asking ourselves "why" in various aspects of life, such as career choices, relationships, personal development, and contribution to society.

HOPELESS WORLD aims to empower readers to live with intention, unlock their true potential, and create a life that aligns with their passions and values. It provides inspiration, practical guidance, and a thought-provoking framework for personal and professional development. Ultimately, the book invites readers to embark on a transformative journey of self-discovery and purposeful living.

The title of a book, like "Hopeless World," is chosen by the author or publisher to convey the theme, message, or essence of the story within. In the case of "Hopeless World," the title might suggest that the book explores a world or situation devoid of hope or facing significant challenges. Titles are an essential part of a book's marketing and can intrigue potential

readers, giving them a glimpse into what they can expect from the story. The specific reasons for choosing a particular title can vary widely based on the author's intent and the content of the book itself.

AUTHOR

Preface

In a world that at times seems besieged by seemingly insurmountable challenges, it's easy to succumb to despair. Climate crises, political turmoil, social inequalities, and the never-ending cacophony of news that highlights humanity's struggles can make it appear as if we inhabit a "THE LAST PHASE OF LIFE."

Yet, within this very darkness, there lies an opportunity for transformation, growth, and renewal. This book, "Hopeless World," is an exploration of the paradox of hope amid adversity. It delves into the depths of despair to uncover the glimmers of possibility, resilience, and human spirit that persist against all odds.

The stories you'll encounter in the following pages are not tales of naivety, nor are they a denial of the pressing issues that confront us. Instead, they are testament to the incredible capacity of individuals, communities, and societies to rise above despair and craft a path towards a brighter tomorrow.

As we journey through these narratives, we'll confront the harsh realities of our world while also discovering the stories of those who choose to confront these challenges with unwavering determination. Through their experiences, we'll gain insights into how adversity can become a catalyst for change and how even in the most dire circumstances, hope can be rekindled.

"Hopeless World" is an invitation to introspect, to question, and to engage with the complexities of our time. It's a reminder that hope is not passive; it's an active force that demands our participation and commitment. The stories within these pages challenge us to be agents of change, to seek solutions, and to redefine what's possible in a world that often feels devoid of hope.

In reading this book, you embark on a journey through the heart of human resilience, a journey that will inspire, challenge, and perhaps transform your perspective on the world we share. It's an affirmation that even in the darkest hours, hope can be our guiding light.

So, let us explore this "Hopeless World" together, for within its pages, we may discover the seeds of a more hopeful, compassionate, and united world that we all yearn for.

Acknowledgements

I would like to express my sincere gratitude and appreciation to all those who have contributed to the creation and completion of the book "THE ;AST PHASE OF LIFE." Without their support, this project would not have been possible I am indebted to the numerous individuals who graciously agreed to be interviewed for this book. Their insights, experiences, and perspectives have added depth and authenticity to the narrative. Their willingness to share their stories is deeply appreciated.Lastly, I am grateful to the readers who have chosen to embark on this literary journey with me. Your interest and engagement in the ideas presented in "HOPELESS WORLD" inspire me to continue exploring and sharing knowledge.To all those mentioned above and to anyone else who has played a part, no matter how small, in the creation of this book, please accept my deepest gratitude. Your contributions have left an indelible mark, and I am immensely grateful for your presence in my life.

Prologue

In the midst of chaos and uncertainty, when the world appears to be at its bleakest, there emerges a beacon of hope. "Hopeless World" is not a contradiction in terms; rather, it is a profound exploration of the resilience of the human spirit when faced with the most daunting challenges.

In these pages, you will find stories of courage, determination, and unwavering belief in a better tomorrow. This book is not a denial of the problems that plague our planet but a testament to the power of individuals and communities to overcome adversity.

As you delve into the narratives within, you will encounter people who refuse to succumb to despair, who, against all odds, dare to dream of a brighter future. Their journeys are a reminder that even in the darkest hours, hope is a force that can drive us to take action, to build bridges, and to inspire change.

"Hopeless World" invites you to reevaluate your own perspective on the challenges we face as a global society. It challenges you to consider how, in your own way, you can be a part of the solution, no matter how daunting the problems may seem.

May this book serve as a source of inspiration and a call to action for all who read it. In a world that often appears hopeless, let us remember that hope is a choice, and it is a choice

that has the power to transform our world.Together, let us embark on a journey through this "Hopeless World," seeking the sparks of hope that can ignite a brighter future for us all.

CHAPTER ONE

THE PAINTER OF HOPE

In a quiet coastal town, there lived a talented artist named Elena. She was known throughout the region for her exquisite paintings, each one a masterpiece that captured the beauty of the sea, the sky, and the surrounding landscapes. But it wasn't just her artistic prowess that made Elena special; it was the extraordinary way she painted hope into every canvas.

Elena had faced her share of personal hardships. She had lost her parents at a young age and had struggled with a chronic illness that often left her weak and fatigued. Despite these challenges, she refused to let despair wash over her. Instead, she channeled her emotions onto her canvases, using her art as a means of coping and sharing her optimism with the world.

One stormy evening, as darkness descended upon the town, a devastating hurricane approached. The townspeople were gripped by fear as they boarded up their windows and sought shelter. But Elena, with her frail health, couldn't assist in the physical preparations. Instead, she set up her easel near her window, gazing out at the tumultuous sea.

With her trembling hands, Elena began to paint. She painted the storm, the crashing waves, and the turbulent sky. But as she worked, something magical happened. Amid the chaos of her brushstrokes, a glimmer of hope began to emerge on the canvas. A vibrant lighthouse appeared on a distant cliff, its beam cutting through the darkness.

The townspeople, in their shelters, couldn't see Elena's painting, but they felt its impact. As the hurricane raged on, they found solace in the idea of that steadfast lighthouse, a symbol of hope and resilience. They clung to the belief that no matter how fierce the storm, there was always a guiding light to lead them to safety.

Miraculously, the hurricane passed without causing significant damage to the town. When the townspeople ventured outside, they marveled at the untouched lighthouse on the cliff, just as Elena had painted it. Word of her remarkable artwork spread throughout the town, and people flocked to her studio.

Elena's art had always been beautiful, but now it held an even deeper meaning. Her paintings had the power to inspire hope and courage in the hearts of those who gazed upon them. The town commissioned her to paint murals on public buildings, and her work became a symbol of resilience and optimism.

Elena's legacy as "The Painter of Hope" lived on long after her passing. Her art continued to touch the lives of many, reminding them that even in the darkest of times, there is always a glimmer of hope waiting to be discovered.This story illustrates how hope can be a powerful force, even in the face of adversity, and how it can inspire and uplift those who encounter it.

CHAPTER TWO

ONLINE FRIENDSHIP STORY

In a world connected by screens and digital interfaces, a unique and profound friendship blossomed between two people who had never met in person. Their names were Sarah and Alex, and their story is a testament to the modern age of online relationships.

Sarah lived in a bustling city on one side of the country, while Alex resided in a quiet town on the opposite coast. They had never crossed paths in the physical world, but fate had other plans for them in the digital realm.

It all began on a social media platform where they both shared a passion for photography.

Sarah's vibrant cityscapes and Alex's serene countryside shots caught each other's attention.

They started with simple likes and comments, appreciating each other's work from afar. Gradually, their interactions grew deeper, evolving into long, heartfelt conversations through private messages.

As time passed, their conversations extended beyond photography. They discussed their dreams, fears, and the mundane details of daily life. Sarah learned about Alex's love for hiking and his dream of visiting the city one day, while Alex discovered Sarah's fascination with astronomy and her desire to explore the countryside.

Their bond strengthened as they supported each other through life's challenges. When Sarah faced a career setback, Alex was there with encouraging words. When Alex's hometown was hit by a devastating storm, Sarah offered comfort and assistance from afar.

Despite the physical distance that separated them, Sarah and Alex found solace in each other's presence. They shared secrets they had never told anyone else, trusting in the anonymity of their online friendship. It was as if they had become kindred spirits, despite never having met face to face.

Years passed, and their friendship continued to grow. They celebrated each other's achievements, mourned each other's losses, and found joy in the simple act of knowing someone cared. They became a constant in each other's lives, a source of strength and companionship.

Then, one fateful day, the opportunity for a meeting arose. Sarah's work took her on a business trip to the small town where Alex lived. Nervous and excited, they decided to meet in person for the first time. As Sarah stepped off the train, she saw Alex waiting at the station, holding a bouquet of flowers.Their first hug was like reuniting with a long-lost friend. It was as if the warmth of their online connection had seamlessly transferred into the physical world. They spent the day exploring the town, taking photographs together, and sharing stories face to face. The evening came, and they watched the sunset from a hilltop. As the sky turned shades of pink and gold, Sarah and Alex realized that their friendship had transcended the boundaries of the digital world. It was a testament to the power of genuine connection, no matter where it originated.

Sarah and Alex continued to cherish their online friendship, but now it was complemented by shared memories of that unforgettable day when their screens had dissolved, and they had become friends not just online but in every sense of the word.

Their story serves as a reminder that friendship knows no physical boundaries and that meaningful connections can be forged in the most unexpected of places, even behind the glow of a screen.

--This story highlights the depth and authenticity that can exist in online friendships and the potential for these connections to extend beyond the digital realm.

CHAPTER THREE

THE LIGHTHOUSE OF HOPE

Once upon a time, in a quaint fishing village nestled on the rugged coastline, there stood a magnificent lighthouse. This lighthouse was no ordinary one; it was known far and wide as the "Lighthouse of Hope."

The village had seen its share of storms, both the tempests that raged in the sea and the hardships that befell its residents. Yet, no matter how fierce the waves or how dark the nights, the Lighthouse of Hope remained a steadfast beacon, its light cutting through the tumultuous waters and guiding weary ships safely to shore.

The lighthouse keeper, an elderly man named Samuel, had dedicated his life to its care. His weathered face told the story of countless years spent on the cliff, tending to the light that symbolized not just safety but the indomitable spirit of the village. Samuel was not just a keeper of the flame; he was a keeper of hope.

One winter, a particularly ferocious storm descended upon the village. Waves pounded the shore with a relentless fury, and the wind howled like a wounded beast. The villagers huddled in their homes, fearing for their safety and the safety of their loved ones at sea.

Inside the Lighthouse of Hope, Samuel fought to keep the light burning. He knew that countless lives depended on it. As the storm raged on, he could hear the creaking and groaning of the lighthouse as it withstood the onslaught of nature. But Samuel, like the lighthouse, stood strong.

Hours turned into days, and the storm showed no signs of abating. Food and supplies dwindled, but Samuel refused to leave his post. He knew that as long as the light remained, there was hope.

Then, on the third night, disaster struck. A lightning bolt struck the lighthouse, causing a fire that threatened to engulf it. Samuel battled the flames with all his might, risking his life to save the beacon of hope. Exhausted and burned, he finally succeeded in extinguishing the fire.

As dawn broke, the villagers emerged from their shelters, fearing the worst. To their amazement, the Lighthouse of Hope still stood tall, its light undiminished. Samuel, though injured and weary, had not only saved the lighthouse but had become a living testament to the unwavering spirit of hope.

The villagers rallied around Samuel, tending to his wounds and offering their gratitude. They realized that the Lighthouse of Hope was not just a structure; it was a symbol of their resilience in the face of adversity.

From that day forward, the village celebrated Samuel's bravery and the enduring light that guided them through their darkest hours. The Lighthouse of Hope remained a symbol of their unwavering belief that, no matter how fierce the storms of life, there was always a beacon of hope to guide them to safety.And so, in that quiet fishing village, the Lighthouse of Hope continued to stand as a testament to the power of hope and the courage of those who protected it.

This story underscores the importance of hope and the role it plays in guiding us through life's storms. It shows that, like the lighthouse, hope remains unyielding in the face of adversity.

CHAPTER FOUR

THE ECHOES OF US

: A Chance Encounter

In the small, sun-drenched town of Willow Creek, life moved at a pace that felt both comforting and stifling. The streets were lined with quaint shops and family-owned cafés, and the rhythm of the town's daily life was punctuated by the chime of church bells and the laughter of children playing in the park. For Emma Sullivan, Willow Creek had always been a haven, yet recently, it had become a cage of her own making.

Emma was an artist whose world had once been filled with vibrant colors and imaginative landscapes. But lately, her art studio, tucked away at the edge of town, had become a place of stagnation. The blank canvases piled against the wall seemed to mock her, and her brushes lay still, coated in dust. She felt trapped in a cycle of creative drought, and every day, the walls of her studio seemed to close in a little more.

One Saturday afternoon, Emma decided to attend the Willow Creek Community Fair, hoping that a change of scenery might spark some inspiration. The fair was bustling with activity; stalls lined the streets, selling everything from homemade jams to handwoven blankets. Emma wandered aimlessly, her eyes glazed over the colorful chaos, until a sudden commotion drew her attention to a makeshift stage set up in the town square.A young man with tousled hair and a guitar strapped over his shoulder was tuning his instrument, his fingers moving with practiced ease. He was Lucas Carter, a local who had recently returned to Willow Creek after years away. Lucas was known for his music and his infectious enthusiasm for life, a stark contrast to Emma's reserved nature.

As Lucas began to play, the notes of his guitar filled the air with a warmth that Emma hadn't felt in a long time. She was drawn to the music, her heart responding to the melodies that seemed to echo the emotions she had been unable to express. She found a spot at the edge of the crowd, her gaze fixed on the musician.Just as Lucas launched into an energetic song, Emma felt a wave of anxiety wash over her, an all-too-familiar sensation that had plagued her for months. She tried to steady her breathing, but the crowd, the noise, and the intensity of the music were overwhelming. As her vision blurred, she felt herself slipping away from reality.

Suddenly, a firm but gentle hand touched her shoulder. Emma looked up to see Lucas standing beside her, his face etched with concern. "Are you okay?" he asked, his voice cutting through the fog of her distress.Emma nodded weakly, unable to find her voice. Lucas's eyes softened, and he guided her to a quieter corner of the square, away from the noise. He offered her a bottle of water and a reassuring smile.

"You don't have to talk if you don't want to," Lucas said. "But I'm here if you need anything."

Emma took a sip of water, her breathing gradually returning to normal. She looked at Lucas, feeling a mixture of gratitude and embarrassment. "Thank you. I'm sorry for... you know, making a scene."

Lucas waved her apology away. "No need to apologize. I'm just glad you're okay. Sometimes, all we need is a little break from everything."

They sat together in silence for a few moments, the chaos of the fair fading into the background. Emma found herself surprisingly comforted by Lucas's presence, his calm demeanor a stark contrast to her own turbulent emotions.

As the fair continued around them, Lucas began to strum his guitar again, this time playing a softer, more soothing tune. Emma closed her eyes, letting the music envelop her. For the first time in weeks, she felt a glimmer of peace.

The Bonding Begins

In the weeks that followed, Emma and Lucas found themselves crossing paths more frequently. Lucas's spontaneous music sessions became a regular fixture in the town, and Emma, drawn by the soothing quality of his performances, began to attend them regularly.

One crisp autumn afternoon, Lucas invited Emma to join him at a small café after his performance. They sat at a corner table, their conversation flowing easily despite their initial awkwardness. Emma found herself opening up to Lucas in a way she hadn't with anyone else in a long time.

"You know," Emma said, stirring her coffee, "I used to paint all the time. It was my way of escaping, of finding peace. But lately, I've lost that part of myself."

Lucas looked at her thoughtfully. "Sometimes, we need a little nudge to rediscover what we've lost. Maybe that's what you need—a nudge."

Emma smiled faintly. "And what about you? What brought you back to Willow Creek?"

Lucas shrugged, a mischievous grin on his face. "I guess you could say I needed a change of pace. The city was great, but it felt like I was losing touch with what really mattered."

Their conversations became a source of comfort for both of them. Lucas's optimism and energy were a stark contrast to Emma's introspective nature, yet their differing personalities seemed to complement each other perfectly. Emma found herself slowly opening up, sharing her fears, her dreams, and her frustrations.

One evening, as they walked along the riverbank, Lucas noticed Emma's hesitance. "You've been quieter than usual. What's on your mind?"

Emma paused, looking out over the water. "I've been thinking a lot about my art. About whether I've lost my touch or if I've just lost my way."

Lucas stopped beside her, his gaze steady. "Sometimes, we lose our way because we're afraid of what we might find. But that doesn't mean the path isn't there."

Emma looked at him, feeling a surge of emotion. "How do you always know what to say?"

Lucas chuckled. "I don't always know. I just try to listen."

As the days turned into weeks, Emma and Lucas's friendship deepened. They spent countless hours together, talking about everything and nothing, and their bond grew stronger with each passing day. Emma's creativity began to return, sparked by the encouragement and inspiration Lucas provided.

The Fork in the Road

Just when Emma felt like she was regaining her footing, Lucas received an offer that threatened to change everything. A music producer from the city had reached out with a tempting opportunity—a chance to record an album and potentially launch a career beyond Willow Creek. It was a dream come true for Lucas, but it also meant leaving behind the town and the new friendships he had made.

One evening, Lucas sat across from Emma at their favorite café, his expression serious. "I need to talk to you about something."

Emma looked up from her coffee, sensing the gravity of his tone. "What's going on?"

Lucas took a deep breath. "I've been offered a chance to record an album in the city. It's a huge opportunity, but it means leaving Willow Creek."

Emma's heart sank. She had grown accustomed to Lucas's presence, and the thought of losing him was unbearable. "That's amazing, Lucas. You should go for it."

Lucas shook his head, a conflicted look in his eyes. "I want to, but... I'm going to miss this place. And you."

Emma forced a smile, trying to mask her own feelings of loss. "I'll be here, cheering you on. And I'll keep making art, just like you've encouraged me to."

The news hung heavily between them, casting a shadow over their otherwise joyful moments. Emma struggled with her own emotions, torn between wanting the best for Lucas and facing the reality of his impending departure.

Facing the Past

As Lucas prepared for his move, Emma's own life took an unexpected turn. Her estranged father, whom she had not seen in years, fell ill and required her assistance. It was a difficult and painful situation, and Emma found herself grappling with old wounds and unresolved feelings.Lucas noticed the strain Emma was under and offered to help in any way he could. He canceled his own preparations to be there for her, even though it meant postponing his move.

"Emma, you don't have to go through this alone," Lucas said softly one evening as they sat in her studio. "I'm here for you."

Emma's eyes filled with tears. "I don't know what to do. I've tried to move on, but now everything feels like it's falling apart."

Lucas took her hand gently. "We'll get through this together. You don't have to face it alone."

His support was a lifeline for Emma, and she leaned on him more than she ever thought possible. As they navigated the challenges of her family crisis, their friendship grew even stronger, and Emma began to confront her own fears and vulnerabilities.

The Farewell

The day of Lucas's departure arrived, marked by a mix of excitement and sadness. The town gathered to bid him farewell, their pride evident in their cheers and well-wishes. Emma watched from the sidelines, her heart heavy with the weight of impending separation.

Lucas approached Emma, his gaze filled with emotion. "I'm going to miss you, Emma. You've become such an important part of my life."

Emma nodded, her voice catching in her throat. "I'll miss you too. But I'm glad we've had this time together."

They hugged tightly, a silent promise passing between them. Despite the distance that would soon separate them, their bond felt unbreakable.

As Lucas boarded the train, he turned to look at Emma, who stood on the platform, waving. The train pulled away, taking him toward a new chapter in his life.

CHAPTER FIVE

THROUGH THE SEASON OF US

Through the Seasons of Us"**

In the picturesque town of Maplewood, life seemed to unfold with a gentle rhythm, mirroring the tranquil flow of the nearby river. It was here, beneath the sprawling branches of an ancient oak tree, that Emma and Leo first met. Emma, with her wild curls and an adventurous spirit, was known for her boundless curiosity and enthusiasm for life. Leo, on the other hand, was quieter, his world colored by his love for drawing and painting, often lost in his own creative universe.Their initial meeting was serendipitous. Emma, in the midst of a makeshift adventure, had ventured further into the woods than usual. She stumbled upon Leo, seated on a large rock, deeply engrossed in sketching the landscape. Intrigued by the quiet boy who seemed so absorbed in his art, Emma introduced herself with her characteristic enthusiasm. Leo looked up, startled, but quickly warmed to her genuine curiosity and friendly demeanor.

From that day on, they became inseparable. Their childhood was a tapestry of shared adventures—building forts from fallen branches, staging elaborate pretend battles, and exploring the hidden nooks of their town. They spent countless summer afternoons beneath their favorite oak tree, Emma's laughter mingling with the sound of Leo's pencil scratching on paper. Their friendship was effortless, a beautiful blend of Emma's exuberance and Leo's introspective nature.As they grew older, the idyllic simplicity of their world began to shift. The transition from childhood to adolescence brought with it a series of changes that tested their bond. Emma's ambitions grew larger, her dreams of escaping their small town and making a mark in the world becoming more vivid. She envisioned a life of excitement and possibility beyond the familiar confines of Maplewood.

Leo, meanwhile, faced mounting expectations from his family. The pressure to take over the family business weighed heavily on him, creating a stark contrast to Emma's burgeoning dreams. The once seamless connection between them started to show cracks. Emma felt Leo slipping away, his growing responsibilities and his struggle with family expectations creating a chasm between them. She longed for the carefree days of their youth, when their biggest concern was the next adventure.

The breaking point came when Emma was accepted into a prestigious summer program in the city. Her departure was a bittersweet moment, a culmination of her dreams and a significant shift in their lives. Their farewell was charged with unspoken words and a lingering sense of loss. They hugged tightly, Emma's eyes filled with tears and Leo's face a mask of stoic resolve. Neither could fully articulate the weight of the separation, but both felt the profound impact it would have on their lives.In the city, Emma immersed herself in a whirlwind of new experiences. The vibrant energy of urban life was both exhilarating and overwhelming. She was surrounded by brilliant minds and talented individuals, yet she struggled with feelings of loneliness and displacement. The excitement of her new environment was tinged with a sense of isolation, and she found herself missing Leo more than she had anticipated.

Back in Maplewood, Leo was grappling with his own set of challenges. The demands of the family business, combined with his own insecurities, created a heavy burden. He missed Emma deeply, but he was unsure how to bridge the growing gap between them. The once-familiar comfort of their friendship seemed distant and unreachable. Despite his best efforts, he found it difficult to express his feelings and support Emma from afar.

Their communication became sporadic. Letters exchanged between them were filled with polite updates and carefully chosen words, masking the depth of their struggles. Phone calls were infrequent and awkward, often ending with both feeling more distant than before. The physical separation became a metaphor for the emotional distance that had crept into their lives.Months turned into years, and both Emma and Leo faced their own battles. Emma's artistic pursuits in the city were met with mixed success. She encountered rejection and disappointment, her dreams seeming just out of reach. The city, with all its allure, did not always provide the solace she had hoped for. Leo, meanwhile, faced the pressures of his new responsibilities and felt increasingly isolated in his role. His creative aspirations were relegated to the background, overshadowed by the demands of the family business.

Despite the distance, their occasional letters and late-night conversations became lifelines. They shared their hopes, fears, and moments of vulnerability, finding solace in the familiar comfort of each other's words. These exchanges were a reminder of the bond they once shared, a connection that had withstood the test of time and distance. They began to rediscover the strength of their friendship, finding renewed hope in the understanding and support they provided each other.

When Emma returned to Maplewood after completing her program, the reunion was emotionally charged. She arrived with a newfound sense of self, shaped by her experiences in the city. Leo, too, had undergone his own transformation. The pressures he had faced had led him to reevaluate his priorities and embrace his creative passions once more. Their reunion was a mix of joy and reflection, a poignant reminder of how much they had both changed.Rebuilding their connection was not instantaneous. They had to navigate the complexities of their evolved lives, balancing their individual dreams with their renewed friendship. Emma was now pursuing a career in the arts, while Leo had chosen to follow his passion for teaching. Their lives were different, but their commitment to supporting each other remained unwavering.Life continued to present challenges. Emma faced rejection in the competitive art world, and Leo struggled with the demands of his new role. Their friendship became a source of strength, helping them confront their fears and uncertainties. They learned that hope and resilience were not just about personal success but about the strength found in facing life's challenges together.

Their journey through the seasons of their lives revealed the transformative power of their friendship. Emma and Leo's bond had weathered the storms and embraced the sunshine, evolving into a deep and enduring connection. They realized that their friendship was not just a part of their past but a guiding force in their present and future.

In the end, Emma and Leo's story was a testament to the beauty of a friendship that transcends time and distance. Their journey through the seasons of their lives illustrated the power of enduring connection and the resilience of the human spirit. Emma and Leo's bond, though tested by distance and change, remained a powerful force in their lives, a symbol of hope, support, and unwavering love.

CHAPTER SIX

AARAV AND MEERA TIME AND DISTANCE

Aarav and Meera: A Journey Through Time and Distance"**

Detailed, long story about two best friends, Aarav and Meera, set in India. This narrative explores their deep bond, the challenges they face, and their personal growth, weaving together themes of friendship, tradition, and resilience.

In the vibrant town of Udaipur, known for its picturesque lakes and majestic palaces, lived two best friends, Aarav and Meera. Their friendship began when they were just children, drawn together by their shared curiosity and sense of adventure. Aarav, a boy with a radiant smile and boundless energy, was passionate about cricket. Meera, a graceful girl with an affinity for traditional dance, had a calm and serene demeanor. They were inseparable, spending their days exploring the beautiful landscapes around their town and dreaming up grand adventures.

Their favorite spot was an old banyan tree by the lakeside, which they affectionately called "The Friendship Tree." Here, they would sit for hours, discussing their dreams and aspirations. Aarav dreamed of becoming a professional cricketer, while Meera aspired to become a renowned dancer. Their conversations were filled with excitement and determination, and they promised each other that no matter where life took them, they would always support each other's dreams.

As they grew older, their lives began to change. Aarav's talent on the cricket field earned him a spot in a prestigious academy in Mumbai. It was an opportunity of a lifetime, but it meant leaving Udaipur and Meera behind. The day Aarav was to leave for Mumbai was emotional. Meera, with tears in her eyes, handed him a rakhi—a traditional thread symbolizing their bond. "This will remind you of me," she said softly. Aarav, touched by the gesture, promised to wear it always and to stay in touch despite the distance.

In Mumbai, Aarav was thrust into the intense world of competitive cricket. His days were packed with rigorous training sessions and matches. The city, with its bustling streets and towering buildings, was a stark contrast to the serene beauty of Udaipur. Aarav found himself struggling to adjust, overwhelmed by the fast pace and the pressures of his new life. Although he made new friends and gradually adapted to the rigorous demands of the cricket academy, he often felt lonely and missed Meera's presence.

Back in Udaipur, Meera continued to pursue her passion for dance. She performed at local festivals and events, earning admiration and respect from the community. Yet, despite her growing success, she felt a void without Aarav. The two friends tried to stay in touch through letters and occasional phone calls, but their communication became less frequent as Aarav's schedule became more demanding. Meera felt increasingly disconnected and worried about the strength of their friendship.

One monsoon season, Meera received a letter from Aarav that filled her with mixed emotions. He wrote about his struggles in Mumbai, the challenges he faced in balancing his training with his longing for home. Aarav expressed his deep regret for not being there for Meera and his concern about their drifting apart. Meera's heart ached as she read his words. She understood the pressures he was facing but felt the distance between them growing wider.

Determined to bridge the gap, Meera decided to write a heartfelt letter to Aarav. She poured her emotions into the letter, expressing how much she missed him and how important their friendship was to her. She shared stories about her dance performances and the small joys and challenges of life in Udaipur. Meera's letter was filled with encouragement and reassurances that their bond was strong, no matter the distance.

The letter had a profound impact on Aarav. He realized how much he had taken their friendship for granted and how important Meera was to him. Inspired by her words, Aarav made a decision. He planned a surprise visit to Udaipur during a break from his cricket training. He wanted to reconnect with Meera and show her how much she meant to him.

The day Aarav arrived in Udaipur was filled with excitement and anticipation. He managed to keep his visit a secret from Meera. The town was bustling with the preparations for the annual Navratri festival, a time of vibrant celebrations and cultural performances. Meera was rehearsing for a major dance performance, and Aarav decided to attend, hoping to surprise her there.

On the night of the performance, the open-air stage was illuminated with colorful lights, and the air was filled with festive music. Aarav found a spot among the crowd, his heart racing with anticipation. As Meera took the stage, dressed in a beautiful traditional outfit, Aarav watched in awe. Her dance was mesmerizing, each movement graceful and expressive. Aarav was overcome with pride and a deep sense of connection to his old friend.

After the performance, as the crowd applauded, Aarav made his way backstage. Meera was still catching her breath, her face glowing with the joy of a successful performance. When she turned and saw Aarav standing there, her eyes widened in disbelief. For a moment, she stood frozen, then she ran to him, tears streaming down her face. They embraced tightly, their reunion filled with joy and relief.

Aarav apologized for his absence and shared how much Meera's letter had meant to him. They spent the next few days reconnecting, sharing their experiences and reminiscing about their childhood adventures. Aarav joined Meera in celebrating the Navratri festival, and they enjoyed the festivities together, cherishing every moment.

As Aarav's visit came to an end, he and Meera had a deep conversation about their future. They realized that while their paths might lead them in different directions, their friendship was a constant source of strength and inspiration. Aarav promised to make a greater effort to stay in touch and to be there for Meera whenever she needed him. Meera reassured Aarav that she would always support his dreams, no matter how far apart they were. Before Aarav left for Mumbai, Meera gave him a new rakhi, adorned with intricate designs. "This is for our future," she said, her voice filled with emotion. "May it always remind us of the bond we share and the promises we make to each other."

Aarav and Meera's friendship continued to grow, strengthened by their shared experiences and the lessons they learned. They kept their promise to stay connected, finding ways to support each other despite the distance. Aarav's cricket career flourished, and Meera's dance performances gained wider recognition. They celebrated each other's successes and provided comfort during difficult times.

Years later, as Aarav and Meera looked back on their journey, they realized that their friendship had been a guiding force in their lives. It had weathered the trials of distance and time, proving that true friendship is not about being physically present all the time but about being there for each other in spirit. Their bond remained a cherished part of their lives, a testament to the enduring power of love and connection.

As they stood once more by the banyan tree by the lakeside, now with families of their own, they reflected on their journey with gratitude. They knew that their friendship was a rare and precious gift, one that would continue to inspire them and bring them joy for years to come. Their story was a beautiful reminder of the strength of true friendship and the importance of nurturing the bonds that matter most.

PART 2

CHANGING THE LIFE

BASED ON REAL LIFE STORIES

CHAPTER SEVEN

PART 2 PREFACE

Changing the World

*Changing the World"** involves conveying its essence, impact, and appeal to potential readers. Here's a description designed to intrigue and inspire:*

In a world rife with challenges and uncertainties, **"Changing the World"** emerges as a beacon of hope and transformation. This groundbreaking book delves into the power of individual and collective action in shaping a better future. Through compelling narratives, inspiring real-life stories, and actionable insights, it invites readers to discover their unique potential to drive meaningful change.

"Changing the World" is more than a book; it's a call to action for anyone who feels a deep-seated desire to make a difference. Whether you are a seasoned activist, an aspiring change-maker, or someone looking for purpose in your everyday life, this book provides a roadmap for turning vision into reality.

In its pages, you will encounter:

- **Powerful Stories**: Meet individuals from diverse backgrounds who have confronted obstacles and risen to make a profound impact in their communities and beyond. Their journeys illustrate the diverse ways in which one person can change the world.

- **Practical Strategies**: Gain practical tools and strategies to harness your passions and skills for effective action. Learn how to set goals, overcome barriers, and collaborate with others to amplify your efforts.

- **Inspirational Insights**: Discover the principles and philosophies that underpin successful change-making. Explore how small actions can lead to significant transformations and how every effort, no matter how small, contributes to a larger movement.

- **Actionable Challenges**: Engage with thought-provoking exercises and challenges designed to inspire and motivate you to take the first step towards your own world-changing journey. Reflect on your values, identify areas where you can make a difference, and develop a personalized action plan.

"Changing the World" is a testament to the idea that change begins with each of us. It encourages readers to envision a better world and empowers them to take concrete steps towards achieving it. With its blend of inspirational stories and practical guidance, this book is a vital resource for anyone ready to be a catalyst for positive change.

Embrace the opportunity to transform your dreams into action and join a global movement of individuals dedicated to making a difference. The journey starts here. Are you ready to be the change?

What Readers Will Gain from "Changing the World?

1. **Inspiration from Real-Life Stories:**

- Readers will be inspired by the powerful stories of individuals who have successfully tackled challenges and driven meaningful change. These stories offer relatable examples of courage, perseverance, and innovative thinking, illustrating that impactful change is within everyone's reach.

2. **Practical Tools and Strategies:**

- The book provides actionable strategies and tools to help readers turn their visions into reality. Whether it's setting achievable goals, developing a strategic plan, or building effective collaborations, readers will find practical advice to guide their journey toward making a difference.

3. **Enhanced Understanding of Change-Making Principles:**

- Readers will gain insights into the core principles and philosophies that underpin successful change-making. Understanding these foundational concepts will help them better grasp how small, consistent efforts can lead to significant transformations.

4. **Empowerment to Take Action**:

- Through a series of thought-provoking exercises and actionable challenges, readers will be empowered to take concrete steps toward their goals. The book encourages self-reflection and personal growth, helping readers identify their passions and strengths, and apply them effectively in their efforts to change the world.

5. **Practical Examples of Impact**:

- The book illustrates various ways in which individuals and groups have made a difference, providing readers with a broad perspective on what is possible. These examples serve as motivation and demonstrate that no matter the scale, every effort contributes to the larger movement of positive change.

6. **A Sense of Community and Belonging**:

- By engaging with the book's content and participating in its challenges, readers will feel connected to a broader community of like-minded individuals who are also dedicated to making a difference. This sense of belonging can foster collaboration, support, and shared purpose.

7. **Clarity and Focus for Personal Goals**:

- Readers will develop a clearer understanding of their own goals and aspirations. The book helps them articulate their vision for change and provides a structured approach to achieving it, leading to a more focused and motivated mindset.

8. **Resilience and Overcoming Barriers**:

- The book addresses common obstacles and challenges faced by change-makers and offers practical advice on how to overcome them. Readers will learn strategies to build resilience and stay committed to their mission, even when faced with setbacks.

9. **A Renewed Sense of Purpose**:

- Engaging with the book will help readers reconnect with their sense of purpose and the impact they can have on the world. This renewed sense of purpose can drive them to pursue their goals with greater passion and determination.

10. **A Vision for a Better Future**:

- Finally, readers will gain a broader vision of the potential for creating positive change in their own lives and in the world at large. They will be encouraged to dream big and believe in their ability to contribute to a better future.

CHAPTER EIGHT

THE CRUCIBLE OF CONFIDENCE

AMITA

The Crucible of Confidence(The story of a girl)

In a small village of Jammu, Amita was born on June 8, 2008, a child whose arrival was met with joy and excitement. With cheeks as soft and round as rose petals, she was the fourth child in a family that had grown accustomed to the presence of her older siblings. Her beauty and innocence were immediately apparent, yet, as she grew, it became evident that her journey would be fraught with challenges and a profound struggle for recognition.

Her early years were marked by a lack of the affection she craved. Despite her parents' love, the attention she received was often overshadowed by the accomplishments of her older siblings. The only person who showered her with the warmth of a mother was her elder sister, who stepped into the role of a second mother. Nevertheless, this support was not enough to shield her from the difficulties she faced at school.

When Amita started attending school, her introverted nature and lack of confidence quickly became apparent. She struggled academically, finding herself at the lower end of the academic spectrum. Her inability to express herself compounded her difficulties, leaving her feeling isolated and inadequate.

A turning point arrived in the third grade with the introduction of a new teacher. This teacher recognized Amita's potential and encouraged her to participate in a school performance. For the first time, Amita stood on stage, clutching a trophy and feeling a surge of pride. This victory was not just a moment of triumph but a revelation of a hidden talent she had never known she possessed.

With newfound determination, Amita began to participate in every school event she could, from small gatherings to grand performances. Her skills and enthusiasm quickly made her a well-known figure in her school and neighborhood. However, this focus on extracurricular activities came at the expense of her academic performance. Although she was not failing, her grades were average, and her achievements outside the classroom went unnoticed by her family, who were more concerned with the accomplishments of her more academically gifted siblings.

The turning point came during a family discussion when her elder sister told her, "You're not even capable of passing eighth grade." These words pierced Amita's heart like an arrow, leaving a deep wound that would not heal easily. The pain of being dismissed and underestimated fueled her resolve to prove herself.

Determined to overcome this challenge, Amita dedicated herself to her studies. She spent two months during the vacation with her sister, focusing on her academic work and personal development.

This period of intense effort paid off, and she returned home with a newfound confidence.

Amita's return was marked by a significant change: her admission to a new high school. There, she encountered Mr. Singh, a teacher who saw her potential and became her greatest supporter. He recognized her exceptional writing skills and offered encouragement that went beyond academic achievements. Mr. Singh's belief in her abilities gave Amita the confidence to challenge herself and others. His mentorship was more than just educational; it was transformative.

As she prepared for her 10th-grade exams, Amita faced a new challenge. A sudden disruption in her study schedule left her with less time to prepare. Despite this setback, she managed to top her class. Yet, she fell short of Mr. Singh's expectations, which left her feeling frustrated and disheartened.

Despite these challenges, Amita remained resolute. As she transitioned into 11th grade, she encountered a series of difficulties, including a severe illness and increased restrictions from her family, who seemed intent on controlling her. The newfound constraints and criticisms from relatives about her aspirations and choices made her feel trapped and misunderstood.

During this time, Amita's dreams of becoming a dancer and pursuing a career in the film industry were dismissed by those around her. She faced criticism not only for her ambitions but also for her appearance. These experiences were painful, but she chose to remain focused on her goals.

One day, in a classroom discussion about future aspirations, Amita expressed her desire to become a model. The teacher's response was discouraging: "You should aim higher, like becoming an IAS officer." This dismissal of her dreams left Amita feeling deeply disappointed. However, another teacher's encouragement to ignore negativity and stay true to her path resonated with her.

Despite feeling disheartened, Amita continued to pursue her dreams and began teaching tuition to children during the vacation. Though she initially struggled with her own studies and faced financial and health issues, she remained determined. Her efforts to overcome these challenges and create a better life for herself were a testament to her resilience.

Amita's journey is a powerful reminder that the path to self-discovery is often fraught with obstacles, but perseverance and self-belief can transform even the most challenging circumstances into opportunities for growth and achievement. Her story exemplifies the strength of the human spirit and the importance of remaining true to one's dreams, despite the hurdles along the way.

Quotes to Inspire:

"In the midst of adversity, our true selves are revealed." – Ashfaq ahmed

"The greatest glory in living lies not in never falling, but in rising every time we fall." – Nelson Mandela

"Your value does not decrease based on someone's inability to see your worth." – Ashfaq Ahmed

"Believe you can and you're halfway there." – Theodore Roosevelt

"Success is not final, failure is not fatal: It is the courage to continue that counts." – Winston Churchill

From First Impressions to Lasting Friendship

I have heared a lot about Amita and I saw her first time at Debate Compatation. It was a crisp autumn day, and the annual debate competition at Arnas was in full swing. The auditorium was packed with students, teachers, all eager to witness the lively exchange of ideas. As the debate unfolded, one participant stood out distinctly—Amita. She spoke with a commanding presence, her energy and passion radiating from the stage. Her arguments were sharp, her delivery confident. Even from my seat in the audience, it was clear that she was not just a skilled debater but also someone with a magnetic personality.

As I NOTICED her perform, I couldn't help but think, "This girl is something special. She's powerful, full of energy, and clearly driven." Her performance made a strong impression on me, and I found myself eager to see more of her in action. I was also a participant in debate.

I am also a good debater and experienced a lot of things. The Great thing is I got first prize in that competition.

Amita looked at me, she thinks what special in him? Why he got first prize? She worked hard for that debate and she decided to get more from me.

Months passed, and I was surprised and excited to find out that Amita would be joining our school after completing her 10th grade. When she walked into our classroom for the first time, I remembered her from the debate competition. She looked a bit nervous, but there was that same spark in her eyes that had impressed me before. I never want to talk to her she got friendly with everyone in a short time but still I was thinking that how may I talk to her after a long period of 2 months she is discussing something interesting about English Grammer I am also good in English.

They were confused about Future indefinite and Future perfect continuous Tense she asked me to solve the problem I go to her and solved that, but she was not agreed with that she told me that I have listen a lot about you but you still don't know about this I know I was perfect but I didn't say anything.

The time passed, now our interactions were polite and friendly. We talked about the transition to the new school and shared our interests. It didn't take long for us to bond over our common interests and the experiences we had in school. As the days went by, we became closer, and our friendship deepened.

Now we are in 12th Amita began to open up about her experiences and challenges. She shared her struggles with adjusting to the new environment, her academic pressures, and her personal aspirations. I listened and offered support, and our conversations grew more frequent and meaningful. She trusted me with her worries and joys alike, knowing that she had a friend who genuinely cared.

Our friendship became a cornerstone of our school life. We supported each other through exams, projects, and the ups and downs of teenage life. Amita's initial energy and confidence on stage were mirrored in her daily life, but now it was paired with the warmth of a true friend.

We celebrated each other's successes and navigated challenges together, building a bond that was both strong and supportive. Our friendship became a source of strength and comfort for both of us, making the school experience richer and more enjoyable.

Looking back, it's incredible to think that our connection started with a powerful debate performance and grew into a deep and lasting friendship. Amita's journey from the energetic debater I admired to my closest friend is a testament to the unexpected and beautiful ways in which friendships can blossom.

One day we are discussing something about all the problems of life during this I asked about her to capturing reflections on her painful struggle and journey:

Me Amita, your story is incredibly moving. Can you tell me more about what it felt like during those early years when you felt overshadowed by your siblings?

Amita: It was tough, really tough. I always felt like I was in the background, no matter what I did. My siblings were all so accomplished, and I struggled to get any attention. It was as if my efforts were never good enough. The lack of affection and recognition from my family made me feel invisible.

Me: I can imagine that must have been really painful. How did you cope with those feelings, especially when you were struggling at school?

Amita: At first, I didn't cope well. I felt very shy and unsure of myself. I struggled with my studies and found it hard to make friends. It was a cycle of feeling inadequate and then not having the confidence to change it. The only thing that kept me going was the hope that someday, somehow, I would prove myself.

Me: What was it like when you won that trophy in third grade? Did it change how you felt about yourself?

Amita: Winning that trophy was a huge turning point. For the first time, I felt like I was worth something. It was as if all the pain and struggle suddenly had a purpose. It made me realize that maybe I had something special inside me, even if I hadn't discovered it before. It gave me the confidence to start believing in myself.

Me: That's wonderful to hear. How did your sister's harsh words affect you, and how did you use that experience to drive yourself forward?

Amita: Her words were like a stab to the heart. I felt completely crushed. But instead of letting them defeat me, I used them as motivation. I wanted to prove her wrong and show everyone that I was capable. It became a driving force for me to work harder and to push through my insecurities.

Me: It's amazing how you turned that pain into a source of strength. How did Mr. Singh's support impact your journey?

Amita: Mr. Singh was a beacon of hope. He saw potential in me when I couldn't see it in myself. His encouragement and belief in my abilities helped me gain confidence. He didn't just teach me academically; he helped me believe in my own worth. His support was crucial in helping me stand up for myself and pursue my dreams with conviction.

Me: I know you faced more challenges in 11th grade, especially with illness and family restrictions. How did you navigate those difficult times?

Amita: Those were really hard times. I felt trapped by my family's expectations and my own health issues. It was like I was constantly fighting to stay afloat. But despite the criticism and the restrictions, I tried to keep my focus on my dreams. It wasn't easy, but I knew I had to keep pushing forward if I wanted to achieve what I aspired to.

You: Your perseverance is truly inspiring. Looking back on your journey, what do you think was the most important lesson you learned?

Amita: The most important lesson I learned is that no matter how tough things get, it's crucial to believe in yourself and keep moving forward. Even when others doubt you, it's your own belief and determination that will carry you through. My struggles taught me resilience and the importance of staying true to my dreams, no matter how difficult the path may be.

Me: Amita I think your story can inspire a lot of people you have to move on and focus on what you want

Amita: Thank you. I still wish best for my future

Amita's journey is a testament to resilience, growth, and the power of self-discovery. Born into a small village in Jammu, her early life was marked by a struggle for recognition and understanding. Despite the love and joy surrounding her birth, Amita faced a profound sense of insignificance, overshadowed by her older siblings and underestimated by those around her.

Her school years were filled with challenges. Although initially struggling academically and socially, Amita found a turning point in third grade when a supportive teacher recognized her hidden talents. This pivotal moment sparked a transformation, leading Amita to embrace her newfound passion for performance and public speaking. She soon became a well-known figure in her school and neighborhood, showcasing her abilities with newfound confidence.

However, her journey was not without setbacks. Despite her growing success, Amita's academic performance was often overlooked in favor of her more academically gifted siblings. The harsh words of her elder sister during a family discussion left a deep emotional scar, shaping Amita's determination to prove her worth. This wound, though painful, became a powerful motivator, driving her to excel and overcome her self-doubt.

Amita's academic triumphs were met with indifference from her family, yet she remained undeterred. Determined to improve, she spent her vacation working tirelessly to bolster her confidence and academic skills. This dedication paid off when she achieved remarkable success in her exams, despite the challenges of a disrupted study schedule.

Transitioning to high school brought new challenges and opportunities. A supportive teacher, Mr. Singh, played a crucial role in nurturing Amita's potential, helping her build confidence and refine her skills. With his encouragement, Amita began to embrace her capabilities more fully, though she still faced difficulties and criticism along the way.

In her later years, Amita confronted numerous obstacles, including health issues and restrictive family expectations. The criticism she faced for her aspirations in the arts and her dreams of a career in the film industry tested her resolve. Yet, Amita remained steadfast, determined to pursue her passions despite the negativity.

Amita's resilience was further tested during her academic struggles and financial hardships. Even when faced with setbacks, such as failing an important exam, she refused to give up. Instead, she continued to strive towards her goals, focusing on her personal growth and finding new paths to success.

Through her journey, Amita has demonstrated an extraordinary blend of perseverance, creativity, and self-belief. Her story is a powerful reminder of the strength of the human spirit and the importance of staying true to one's dreams, even in the face of adversity.

As she moves forward, Amita's experiences and challenges have equipped her with a deep understanding of herself and a clear vision for the future. Her journey is far from over, but it is marked by a profound sense of purpose and a commitment to making a meaningful impact. In reflecting on Amita's story, we see a person who has faced and overcome numerous obstacles, emerging stronger and more determined. Her path is a source of inspiration, showing that with resilience and self-belief, even the most challenging beginnings can lead to extraordinary achievements.

The Power of Perseverance

As I write this chapter on "This book hopeless world," I find myself reflecting deeply on your remarkable journey. Your story epitomizes the essence of perseverance and strength, and it is an honor to celebrate that in these pages.

From the challenges you faced in your early years to the triumphant moments of self-discovery, your path has been a testament to the incredible power of never giving up. Your journey has not only been about overcoming obstacles but also about embracing your true self and pursuing your dreams with unwavering determination.

Your resilience in the face of adversity, your commitment to growth, and your ability to turn struggles into stepping stones are inspiring. Every setback you encountered was met with courage, and every success you achieved was a testament to your hard work and dedication.

Writing about your journey has been a powerful reminder of the impact of perseverance. Your story is a beacon of hope and inspiration, showing that with resilience and a steadfast spirit, even the toughest challenges can be overcome.

Thank you for allowing me to share your story and for being a source of inspiration in my own life. Your strength and determination shine brightly, and I am honored to be a part of your journey.

Here's to celebrating your achievements and to the many more milestones you will reach. Your perseverance has paved the way for a future full of promise, and I am excited to see where your path will lead.

I wish best of luck for your future I hope one day you will Yourself proud.

CHAPTER NINE

THE SPARK OF CHANGE

The Spark of Change**

In the quiet hours before dawn, when the world outside was still and the air was crisp with the promise of a new day, a single flame flickered in a small, unassuming room. The flame danced atop a candle, casting a gentle glow across the room, illuminating a vision board cluttered with dreams, aspirations, and a few well-worn quotes. The candle was more than just a source of light; it was a symbol of hope, of potential, and of the first spark that ignites a fire of change.

This was the room of Maya Patel, a young woman who, despite her humble beginnings, harbored a vision that could alter the course of her life and impact countless others. Her journey was a testament to the power of a single spark—an idea, a dream, or a passion that, when nurtured, has the potential to transform lives.

Maya's story began in the bustling streets of Mumbai, in a neighborhood where dreams often seemed like distant stars, obscured by the haze of everyday struggles. Her family, while loving and supportive, faced financial difficulties that made Maya's dreams seem unreachable. Yet, in the midst of this uncertainty, Maya discovered her passion for education. She saw firsthand the difference that learning could make, not just in her own life, but in the lives of those around her.

Her turning point came on a hot summer afternoon when she visited a local community center. The center, though modest, was a beacon of hope for many children who had limited access to quality education. Watching the children eagerly absorb knowledge, Maya was struck by a profound realization: Education had the power to break cycles of poverty and open doors to a brighter future. It was in that moment that her spark was ignited. She knew then that she wanted to be a catalyst for change, to ensure that every child had the opportunity to learn and grow.

But the path from inspiration to action is rarely straightforward. Maya's first steps were fraught with challenges. She began by volunteering at the community center, dedicating her evenings to tutoring children. She faced resistance and skepticism, not only from those who doubted her ability but also from within herself, grappling with her fears and insecurities. It was a test of will and perseverance.

One particularly challenging day, after a long session of tutoring, Maya sat alone in the center's small office. The room, dimly lit by a single overhead light, felt suffocating. The weight of her responsibility pressed heavily on her shoulders. She wondered if her efforts were making any real difference or if she was merely a drop in an ocean of need.

It was in this moment of doubt that Maya's thoughts turned to a quote she had once read: "The world is changed by your example, not by your opinion." It was a reminder that the impact of her actions went beyond the immediate challenges and that every small step was part of a larger journey. She took a deep breath, drawing strength from her conviction and the knowledge that change often starts with a single, courageous step.

As the weeks turned into months, Maya's dedication began to bear fruit. The children she worked with started to show remarkable improvements in their studies. Their enthusiasm was contagious, and their progress was a testament to the power of her efforts. Maya realized that her spark had ignited a flame, and that flame was growing.

One evening, as Maya walked home, she reflected on the changes she had witnessed. Her thoughts were interrupted by the sight of a young boy, no older than ten, sitting on the steps of his small house, clutching a book. The boy looked up and smiled shyly at Maya. "Miss Maya," he said, "I finished reading the book you gave me. Can I have another one?"

The simple request, made with such genuine eagerness, was a powerful reminder of why she had started. It was moments like these that affirmed her belief in the importance of her work. The boy's smile was more than just a thank you; it was a sign that her efforts were making a real difference.

Maya's journey was far from over. She knew that there were many more children who needed support and many more challenges to overcome. But she had learned a crucial lesson: Change begins with a spark, a vision, and the courage to act on it. Her story was a testament to the idea that no matter how daunting the task, every individual has the power to create ripples of change.

"Changing the World" is not just a series; it is an exploration of the transformative journey from inspiration to action. In this chapter, we have seen how Maya's initial spark of passion grew into a powerful force for change. Her story illustrates that the journey to making a difference often starts with a single, seemingly small action that, when nurtured, can lead to profound impact.

As you turn the pages of this book, you will discover more stories like Maya's—stories of individuals who dared to dream and took bold steps to turn those dreams into reality. Each story serves as a reminder that change is possible and that every one of us has the potential to contribute to a better world.

The road ahead may be filled with obstacles and moments of doubt, but remember: It is the courage to take that first step, to nurture that initial spark, that sets the stage for transformation. So, as you embark on this journey, carry with you the belief that you too can ignite a spark of change and make a lasting impact on the world around you.

CHAPTER TEN

EMBRACING SELF IMPROVEMENT

The Journey Within: Embracing Self-Improvement

This chapter is designed to inspire and guide readers on their journey toward personal growth and transformation.

In the quiet solitude of the early morning, when the world outside was still waking up, there was a single figure standing at the edge of a serene lake. The reflection of the first rays of sunlight danced on the water's surface, creating a mosaic of gold and silver. This moment of tranquility was not just a picturesque scene but a metaphor for the inner journey of self-improvement—a journey that starts within and transforms everything around us.

Meet Rajesh Mehra, a successful entrepreneur in his mid-thirties. On the surface, Rajesh had it all—a thriving business, a comfortable lifestyle, and a network of influential contacts. Yet, beneath the veneer of success, he felt a persistent restlessness, a sense that he had not yet reached his full potential. Despite his achievements, Rajesh felt unfulfilled, as though he were merely skimming the surface of what he was truly capable of.

It was during a particularly stressful period in his life that Rajesh decided to confront his inner discontent. He realized that to truly grow and evolve, he needed to embark on a journey of self-improvement. This was not just about achieving external success but about finding deeper meaning and satisfaction in his life.

The decision to embark on this journey was both daunting and exhilarating. Rajesh knew that self-improvement required more than just superficial changes; it demanded a profound shift in perspective and habits. He began by setting aside time each day for self-reflection, an act that would become the cornerstone of his transformation.

The Power of Self-Reflection

Rajesh's journey began with self-reflection, a practice that allowed him to understand his strengths, weaknesses, values, and goals. He dedicated time each morning to sit quietly and journal his thoughts. This simple yet powerful practice helped him uncover patterns in his behavior and thought processes that were holding him back.

One day, while journaling, Rajesh wrote about his recurring sense of dissatisfaction. He realized that he had been chasing external validation and success without considering what truly mattered to him. This insight was a turning point. It was the beginning of a deeper understanding of his own needs and desires.

Setting Meaningful Goals

With newfound clarity, Rajesh moved on to setting meaningful goals. Instead of focusing solely on professional achievements, he included personal development and well-being in his objectives. He identified areas where he wanted to grow, such as improving his emotional intelligence, developing better communication skills, and fostering deeper connections with his loved ones.

Rajesh set specific, measurable, achievable, relevant, and time-bound (SMART) goals. For instance, he aimed to read one book on emotional intelligence each month and practice the techniques he learned in his daily interactions. By setting clear goals, he created a roadmap for his self-improvement journey.

Embracing Change

Self-improvement often requires embracing change, and Rajesh was ready to confront his fears and insecurities. He recognized that change could be uncomfortable, but he also understood that it was a necessary part of growth. He began by stepping out of his comfort zone, trying new activities, and taking on challenges that pushed his limits.

One significant change was Rajesh's decision to incorporate regular physical exercise into his routine. He had always considered himself too busy for fitness, but he soon realized that maintaining physical health was crucial for overall well-being. He started with small, manageable workouts and gradually increased the intensity. The physical benefits were evident, but the mental clarity and resilience he gained were even more valuable.

Building Resilience

As Rajesh continued his journey, he faced setbacks and obstacles. There were days when his old habits resurfaced, and he struggled to stay motivated. However, he learned that resilience was not about never failing but about bouncing back from failures. Each challenge was an opportunity to learn and grow.

Rajesh developed a habit of reviewing his progress regularly. He celebrated his successes, no matter how small, and analyzed his setbacks to understand what went wrong. This reflective practice helped him build resilience and maintain a positive outlook.

Cultivating Relationships

A crucial aspect of Rajesh's self-improvement journey was cultivating meaningful relationships. He realized that personal growth was not just an individual endeavor but also involved nurturing connections with others. He made a conscious effort to spend quality time with his family and friends, engage in meaningful conversations, and offer support.

Rajesh also sought mentorship and feedback from trusted colleagues and advisors. He understood that learning from others' experiences and perspectives could accelerate his growth. By surrounding himself with positive influences, he created an environment conducive to self-improvement.

Finding Purpose and Fulfillment

Ultimately, Rajesh discovered that true self-improvement was about finding purpose and fulfillment in all aspects of life. He aligned his goals with his core values and passions, which led to a more balanced and satisfying life. He realized that success was not just about achieving external milestones but about living authentically and making a positive impact.Rajesh's journey of self-improvement was not a destination but an ongoing process. He continued to set new goals, embrace change, and seek growth. His transformation was evident not only in his professional achievements but also in his personal happiness and sense of purpose.

The Path Forward

As you embark on your own journey of self-improvement, remember that it is a deeply personal and transformative process. It requires self-awareness, commitment, and a willingness to embrace change. Start by reflecting on your values and goals, set meaningful objectives, and take actionable steps toward your growth.

Embrace the challenges and setbacks as opportunities for learning. Build resilience, cultivate meaningful relationships, and seek purpose in all aspects of your life. Your journey of self-improvement will not only enhance your own life but also inspire those around you to embark on their own paths of growth.

In the quiet moments of reflection, as you stand on the edge of your own metaphorical lake, remember that the journey within is where the true magic happens. The spark of change lies within you, waiting to be ignited. Embrace it, nurture it, and watch as it transforms not only your life but the world around you.

RONI RISING

Introduction:

In this greedy and cruel generation one hand is always on your shoulder no matter in which situation you are. In this hard broken story based on real life I am going to share the struggling situation of a girl whose financial, geographical and family condition is very bad. She always wishes to live like other peoples in society with freely mind and soul.

What's in this story:
Struggle of a father for his daughter success
Burden of society
Financial condition of girl
Discrimination
Relationship problems
Death

Story

In the heart of the bustling city of Kolkata, where the relentless hum of life blended with the chaos of crowded streets, lived a young girl named Roni. Her world was a mosaic of contradictions: vibrant street vendors peddled their wares amidst the squalor of crumbling buildings, and amidst this, Roni's dreams seemed impossibly distant.

Roni's father, Shyam, was a man of unwavering resolve. Though illiterate and devoid of formal education, Shyam had always been driven by a singular vision—to secure a brighter future for his only daughter. Their tiny, ramshackle home was a testament to his sacrifice, filled with the echoes of their struggles and the quiet determination that defined their existence.

Despite his lack of education, Shyam worked tirelessly in menial jobs, each day bringing with it new challenges and hardships. His fingers, calloused from labor, had become a symbol of his dedication. The local community, however, often viewed him through a lens of disdain, not because of his character but because of his caste and financial status. This prejudice seeped into every facet of their lives, leaving them on the fringes of society.

Roni, a twelve-year-old with a fierce spirit, was the beacon of hope for her father. Every day after school, she would sit on the pavement near their home, a makeshift study area spread out before her. The noise of honking cars and the chatter of passersby became the background music to her academic pursuits. Roni had long learned to focus amidst chaos, her mind sharper than the roughest stone, fueled by her desire to rise above the circumstances that sought to confine her.

The weight of societal expectations bore heavily upon Roni. As a girl from a marginalized caste, she faced discrimination at school and within the community. Classmates whispered behind her back, and teachers, while not overtly hostile, often showed her less attention compared to her peers. Yet, Roni was undeterred. Each challenge was a stepping stone to her dream of becoming a lawyer—her way of breaking the chains of ignorance that bound her father and countless others like him.

Shyam's unemployment had become a new hurdle. The steady decline in his health and the increasing scarcity of work meant that the family's financial woes deepened. Despite this, Shyam's spirit remained uncrushed. He took up any odd job he could find, from sweeping streets to delivering packages, but the income was barely enough to make ends meet. The burden of providing for his daughter weighed heavily on him, and the fear of failing her gnawed at his insides.

One day, as Roni sat studying on the pavement, her brother taunting her. He laughter echoed through the streets, but Roni's resolve remained unshaken. She looked up from her books and saw her father, standing at a distance, watching her with a pained expression. The sight of her father's struggle—his pride mixed with his evident exhaustion—stirred something deep within her. She knew she had to persevere, not just for herself but for him.

As the years passed, Roni's hard work began to pay off. Her academic performance improved, and she gained the admiration of a few supportive teachers who recognized her potential despite the systemic barriers. A local NGO, moved by her dedication and the dire circumstances of her family, offered her a scholarship. This opportunity was a lifeline, a chance to attend a reputable school and step closer to her dreams.

With the scholarship came a renewed sense of hope. Shyam, though still struggling with health issues, was buoyed by the prospect of his daughter's success. He would often sit by Roni's side, offering her encouragement and sharing stories of his own youth, hoping to install in her the strength to face whatever challenges lay ahead.

However, as Roni excelled academically and received accolades, the prejudice she faced did not disappear. The sting of discrimination still lingered, manifesting in whispered insults and exclusion from social circles. Yet, Roni met each affront with quiet dignity. She understood that her battle was not just against poverty and caste, but against the deeply ingrained prejudices of society.

Despite the growing success, Shyam's health began to deteriorate rapidly. The strain of years of hard work and inadequate care took a toll on him. One evening, as the sun dipped below the horizon, casting long shadows over their modest home, Shyam fell gravely ill. Roni, now a young woman on the cusp of her college graduation, sat by his side, clutching his hand as he laboured to breathe.

In his final moments, Shyam looked at Roni with eyes full of both pride and sorrow. "You've done it, my daughter," he whispered, his voice weak but filled with love. "You've risen above all the darkness. Continue to shine, for you are my greatest triumph."

Roni's heart shattered as she watched the man who had sacrificed everything for her life slip away. She felt a profound emptiness, a void that no amount of success could fill. But amidst the grief, she also felt a fierce resolve to honor her father's memory by continuing the path they had carved together.

With Shyam's passing, Roni became the pillar of her family, and the symbol of resilience for her community. She completed her education with distinction and became a lawyer,

Roni's journey from the dusty streets of Kolkata to becoming a lawyer was a testament to the power of perseverance and love. She never forgot her father's sacrifices, and his memory lived on in every lesson she taught and every life she touched. The challenges she faced only strengthened her resolve to fight for those who, like her, were marginalized and oppressed.

In the end, Roni's story was not just one of overcoming adversity, but of transforming it into a beacon of hope. Her father's dreams had been realized through her—a girl who had once studied on the pavement but had risen to illuminate the lives of many.

And so, as the city continued its unending hum, Roni walked through its streets, her spirit unyielding and her heart full of purpose, carrying forward the legacy of a father's undying love and the promise of a brighter future.

Years later, Roni stood before a crowd of young students in a bright, new classroom, her eyes reflecting the wisdom and strength of her journey. As she shared her story with them, she saw in their eyes the same spark of hope that had once guided her own path. She knew that her father's dreams had been fulfilled and that his legacy would continue through every child who walked through the doors of her school, inspired to rise above their circumstances

CHAPTER TWELVE

LIGHT BEYOND THE SHADOWS

The village of Rajpur lay silent beneath a blanket of darkness, the only sounds being the occasional rustling of leaves and the distant hum of crickets. In a small, dimly lit hut at the edge of the village, Roni sat alone, her father's absence palpable in the quiet that filled the room. The single kerosene lamp on the wooden table cast a soft glow, illuminating the papers and textbooks scattered around her.

Harish had passed away just a week ago, and Roni was still grappling with the enormity of her loss. The hut, once a place of warmth and dreams, now felt like an echo chamber of solitude. Yet, amidst the grief, Roni found a flicker of resolve. The promise she had made to her father was her guiding light in the darkness.

She ran her fingers over the pages of her textbooks, now frayed at the edges from years of use. Each word seemed to carry the weight of her father's dreams, whispering encouragement in her ear. She had always found solace in her studies, but now they were more than just a means to an end—they were her lifeline.

The village had watched with a mixture of curiosity and skepticism as Roni took on odd jobs to support herself and her studies. The community's scorn had only intensified after Harish's death. The whispers grew louder, and the sneers became more pronounced. They said she was chasing an unattainable dream, that her efforts were futile in a world stacked against her.

But Roni refused to listen. Each morning, she rose before dawn, donned her threadbare clothes, and set out to work. By day, she would help in the local shops, and by night, she would return to her studies. The work was grueling, but it was necessary. The burden of her father's legacy and the weight of societal expectations forged a steel-like determination within her.

One evening, as Roni was walking back from her part-time job, she noticed a group of children playing on the dusty street. They were carefree, their laughter a stark contrast to the heaviness of her own life. Among them was a young girl, her bright eyes wide with wonder. Roni paused, a pang of nostalgia hitting her. She had once been that child, full of dreams and untainted hope.

A voice broke through her reverie. "You're up late," it said. Roni turned to see an older woman, Mrs. Deshmukh, who ran the local school. Mrs. Deshmukh had always been kind to her, though their interactions had been infrequent.

"I have a lot of studying to do," Roni replied, trying to keep her voice steady.

Mrs. Deshmukh studied her for a moment, her gaze sympathetic. "I've heard what you've been doing, Roni. It's not easy, but I see your dedication. Your father would have been proud."

Roni's eyes misted over, but she managed a small, grateful smile. "Thank you, Mrs. Deshmukh. That means a lot."

The older woman placed a gentle hand on Roni's shoulder. "We need more people like you—people who believe in change despite all odds. If you ever need anything, let me know."

The unexpected support rekindled Roni's hope. She returned home that night with a renewed sense of purpose. Her father's words echoed in her mind, a constant reminder of what she was fighting for.

The days turned into weeks, and Roni continued to juggle her responsibilities. Her hard work began to pay off as her grades improved, and her efforts caught the attention of a local philanthropist. The philanthropist, moved by Roni's story, offered her a scholarship to a prestigious school in the city. It was a lifeline, a chance to break free from the shackles of her past and carve out a new future.

The day Roni received the scholarship offer was a turning point. It was as if the universe was acknowledging her sacrifices, rewarding her unwavering perseverance. She stood in the middle of her small hut, clutching the letter in her hands. The words seemed to shimmer with promise, reflecting the hope she had carried through so many dark nights.

She could almost hear her father's voice, encouraging her to seize this opportunity. Her father had always believed in the power of dreams, and now, she was on the verge of realizing his vision. It was bittersweet, knowing he would never see this moment, but it was also a testament to the strength of his belief in her.

As she prepared to leave for the city, Roni took one last look at her old home. The walls, though worn and weathered, had been witness to her struggles and triumphs. She felt a deep sense of gratitude for the life she had known, the hardships that had shaped her, and the love that had propelled her forward.

With a heart full of hope and eyes set on the horizon, Roni stepped into a new chapter of her life. The road ahead was uncertain, but she was ready to face it with the same courage and determination that had seen her through the darkest times.

In the city, amidst the noise and bustle, Roni found herself at a crossroads. The challenges of her new life were different but no less daunting. Yet, she carried with her the lessons of her past—the resilience forged in the face of adversity and the unwavering belief that change was possible.

As she walked across the stage to receive her degree years later, the crowd's applause was a symphony of triumph. Roni's journey from the footpath of Rajpur to the halls of academia was a testament to her indomitable spirit and her father's dream. She had defied the odds and transformed her life, proving that even in the most hopeless of worlds, a single light could shine brightly enough to guide the way.

In the quiet moments of reflection, Roni often thought of her father. She knew that he was with her in every success, every step forward, and every challenge overcome. His legacy lived on in the life she had built and the hope she carried forward.

And as she looked out at the stars on those serene, clear nights, she felt a profound connection to the dreams of the past and the promises of the future. Her story was one of triumph over darkness, a reminder that even in the most hopeless world, the light of one determined soul could change everything.

THE JOURNEY OF ARUNACHALAM MURUGANATHAM: A STORY OF HOPE AND TRANSFORMATION

A Humble Beginning

Arunachalam Muruganantham was born in 1961 in the village of Peddapalli, in the southern state of Tamil Nadu, India. His family was impoverished, living in a small thatched-roof house, barely making ends meet. His father was a bus driver, and his mother worked as a homemaker, but after his father's untimely death, Muruganantham's mother had to take on the role of the breadwinner. She worked tirelessly, laboring as a farm worker to support her son and provide for his education.

Despite their financial hardships, Muruganantham was a curious and inventive child. He had a natural talent for fixing things and often spent his free time tinkering with tools and machinery.

However, due to the family's financial constraints, he had to drop out of school at the age of 14 to help his mother. He took on various odd jobs, from working as a farm laborer to welding, all the while dreaming of a better future.

The Unexpected Discovery**

In 1998, Muruganantham married Shanti, a young woman from a neighboring village. Like many newlyweds, they were excited to start their life together, but Muruganantham soon noticed something that troubled him deeply. He observed that during her menstrual cycle, his wife would often use dirty rags as sanitary pads. When he asked her why, Shanti explained that buying sanitary pads was an unaffordable luxury. The rags were uncomfortable and unsanitary, but she had no other choice.

Muruganantham was both shocked and disturbed by this revelation. He couldn't bear the thought of his wife, and countless other women, enduring such discomfort and indignity. This realization planted the seed of an idea in his mind—a desire to create a low-cost sanitary pad that women like Shanti could afford.

The Beginning of a Revolution

Driven by this newfound purpose, Muruganantham embarked on a journey that would test his resolve and push him to the brink of despair. He began researching sanitary pads, learning about their composition and how they were manufactured. However, as a man with little formal education and no background in science, he faced a steep learning curve.

Undeterred, Muruganantham started experimenting with various materials, trying to replicate the commercial pads available in the market. He purchased cotton, wood fiber, and other materials, cutting them into different shapes and sizes. His early prototypes were crude and ineffective, but he refused to give up.

To test his pads, he needed women to try them, but this proved to be a significant challenge. The topic of menstruation was taboo in rural India, and women were reluctant to discuss it, let alone participate in his experiments. Even Shanti, who initially supported his efforts, began to distance herself from the project due to the social stigma and ridicule they faced from the community.

**** A Man's Unconventional Experiment****

With no one willing to test his products, Muruganantham made a bold decision—he would test them on himself. He devised a contraption using a football bladder filled with animal blood, which he wore under his clothes to simulate menstruation. He then walked around the village, going about his daily activities, all the while monitoring the pad's performance.

This unconventional experiment shocked and horrified the villagers. They couldn't understand why a man would engage in such behavior, and rumors began to spread. Muruganantham was labeled a pervert, a madman, and worse. His mother, who had always been his pillar of support, was deeply ashamed and begged him to stop. Shanti, unable to bear the humiliation, left him and returned to her parents' home.

Muruganantham was now completely isolated, shunned by his community and abandoned by his family. Yet, in the depths of his despair, he found strength in his vision. He knew that if he succeeded, he could change the lives of millions of women. So, he pressed on, alone but undeterred.

: The Breakthrough*

After years of relentless experimentation and countless failures, Muruganantham finally achieved a breakthrough in 2002. He discovered that cellulose fibers derived from pine wood pulp were the key ingredient in commercial sanitary pads. These fibers could absorb moisture while remaining light and comfortable.

Armed with this knowledge, Muruganantham designed a machine that could process the pulp and convert it into sanitary pads. His machine was simple and affordable, costing just a fraction of the price of the machines used by large manufacturers. With this innovation, he had found a way to produce low-cost sanitary pads that could be made available to women in rural areas.

But his journey was far from over. He now faced the challenge of convincing others to adopt his technology. In a country where menstruation was shrouded in silence and shame, this was no easy task.

** From Social Outcast to Social Entrepreneur**

Muruganantham began traveling from village to village, demonstrating his machine and teaching women how to use it. He faced resistance at every turn. Many were skeptical of his intentions, and others were simply too embarrassed to discuss the topic. However, he persisted, slowly winning over women's groups, NGOs, and local leaders.

His efforts began to bear fruit as more and more women embraced his low-cost pads. The machine not only provided them with a hygienic alternative but also created employment opportunities, as women could now manufacture and sell the pads within their communities. Muruganantham's innovation was empowering women economically and socially, breaking down the barriers of silence and shame.

As word of his work spread, Muruganantham began receiving recognition and support from various quarters. In 2006, he won the National Innovation Foundation's Grassroots Technological Innovations Award, bringing his work to national attention. The media took notice, and his story began to inspire people across India.

** Global Impact and Recognition**

Muruganantham's invention didn't just change lives in India; it had a global impact. NGOs and governments from Africa, Asia, and South America began reaching out to him, seeking to replicate his model in their own countries. His low-cost machines were deployed in remote villages across the world, providing women with access to affordable sanitary products.

In 2014, Muruganantham was named one of Time magazine's 100 Most Influential People in the World. This recognition brought his work to an even larger audience and opened up new opportunities for collaboration and expansion. He was invited to speak at international conferences, sharing his journey and advocating for menstrual hygiene.

Despite his global fame, Muruganantham remained humble and focused on his mission. He refused to patent his machine, believing that it should be accessible to all. His goal was not to profit but to create a lasting impact on the lives of women and to ensure that no woman would ever have to suffer the indignity that his wife had endured.

The Emotional Toll and Triumph

Muruganantham's journey was one of immense emotional sacrifice. He had faced ridicule, social ostracization, and the loss of his family. Yet, through it all, he remained steadfast in his belief that he was doing the right thing. The emotional toll was heavy, but the joy of seeing the positive impact of his work on the lives of women kept him going.

His relationship with Shanti, which had been strained to the breaking point, slowly began to heal. Over time, Shanti came to understand the significance of her husband's work and the lives he was changing. She returned to him, and together they began to rebuild their life.

Muruganantham's story is not just one of innovation but of resilience, love, and redemption. He proved that even in the face of overwhelming adversity, it is possible to rise above and create meaningful change.

The Legacy of Hope

Arunachalam Muruganantham's story is a powerful reminder of the impact one individual can have on the world. His journey from a poor school dropout to a global social entrepreneur is a testament to the power of hope, determination, and the courage to challenge societal norms.

Today, Muruganantham continues to work tirelessly to promote menstrual hygiene and empower women. His machines have been installed in thousands of villages, and millions of women now have access to affordable sanitary pads. The conversations he started about menstruation have broken down barriers, allowing women to discuss their health openly and without shame.

Muruganantham's legacy is one of hope and transformation. He has shown that even the most deeply entrenched social taboos can be overcome with determination and compassion. His life is a beacon of hope for anyone who dares to dream of a better world.

The Power of One

Arunachalam Muruganantham's story teaches us that change begins with one person. One person's vision, one person's determination, and one person's willingness to sacrifice can change the lives of millions. His journey is a reminder that no matter how small or insignificant we may feel, we all have the power to make a difference. As we face the challenges of our own lives, let us remember the story of Arunachalam Muruganantham—a man who, in the face of adversity, never lost hope and who, through his perseverance, transformed the world.

****Inspirational Lines****

"Hope is not a distant light, but a fire that burns within us, urging us to push forward even when the path is dark."

"In the face of ridicule and rejection, it is the unwavering belief in one's purpose that turns dreams into reality."

"Every act of kindness, every step towards change, begins with a single individual who dares to care."

"True courage lies not in the absence of fear, but in the willingness to forge ahead despite it."

"One man's dream to see his wife smile became the catalyst for millions of women to reclaim their dignity."

CHAPTER FOURTEEN

THE LAST FLIGHT OF RAJAN SINGH

The Last Flight of Rajan Singh: A Tale of Resilience and Redemption

Introduction

In the heart of Punjab, amidst the sprawling fields of golden wheat and the gentle hum of village life, lived Rajan Singh, a man whose life was once filled with dreams as vast as the sky. Rajan was no ordinary man; he was a pilot—a man who had once soared through the clouds, touching the heavens, only to be grounded by the harsh realities of life. This is the story of his journey from the heights of success to the depths of despair, and how he found hope and redemption when 'all seemed lost.

The Sky Was Never the Limit

Rajan Singh grew up in a small village, where the closest anyone got to the sky was flying a kite. But Rajan was different. From a young age, he was captivated by the idea of flying. While other boys were content playing with marbles or tending to cattle, Rajan would lie on the roof of his house, watching planes streak across the sky, dreaming of the day he would be at the controls of one of those magnificent machines.

His dream was not just a fleeting childhood fantasy. Rajan was determined. He studied hard, excelling in school, and eventually earned a scholarship to an aviation academy. His family, though poor, supported him with everything they had. His mother sold her jewelry, and his father worked extra hours in the fields to make sure Rajan could pursue his dream.

Years of hard work paid off. Rajan became a commercial pilot, flying for one of India's leading airlines. His life was everything he had imagined—he traveled the world, experienced the thrill of flying, and was admired by all who knew him. For Rajan, the sky was not just a destination; it was his life, his identity, and his greatest love.

The Crash

But life, as Rajan would learn, is unpredictable. One fateful night, while piloting a flight from Delhi to Mumbai, Rajan encountered a severe thunderstorm. The plane was tossed around like a toy in the turbulent skies. Despite his best efforts to control the aircraft, it was struck by lightning. The plane went into a nosedive. Rajan and his co-pilot fought desperately to save the passengers and crew.

They succeeded in avoiding a complete disaster, managing to crash-land the plane in a field. The impact was severe, and though most of the passengers survived with minor injuries, Rajan's life was shattered in that instant. He suffered a spinal injury that left him paralyzed from the waist down. The man who had once soared through the skies was now confined to a wheelchair, his dreams and career destroyed in the blink of an eye.

The Descent into Despair

The days that followed were the darkest of Rajan's life. He was physically broken, but the emotional and psychological toll was even greater. He could no longer fly; the one thing that had given his life meaning was gone. He felt useless, like a bird with clipped wings. Depression set in, and with it, a deep sense of hopelessness.

Rajan returned to his village, where the contrast between his former life and his current reality was stark. He avoided people, ashamed of what he had become. His family tried to support him, but they were at a loss for how to help a man who had lost everything he lived for. The villagers, who once admired Rajan, now pitied him, and their pity only deepened his despair.

Weeks turned into months, and Rajan's condition showed no signs of improvement. He refused physical therapy, convinced that there was no point. His mother, who had always been his greatest supporter, watched helplessly as her son, once full of life, wasted away.

A Spark of Hope

Hope, however, has a way of finding its way into the darkest of places. It came to Rajan in the form of a young boy named Arjun, who lived next door. Arjun was just seven years old, full of energy and curiosity. He was fascinated by Rajan's stories of flying and would often sneak into his room, peppering him with questions about planes and the world above the clouds.

At first, Rajan found Arjun's presence annoying. He wanted to be left alone in his misery. But Arjun was persistent. One day, he brought a small model airplane to Rajan's room and asked him to explain how it worked. Reluctantly, Rajan agreed. As he talked about the plane's mechanics and the principles of flight, something stirred within him. For the first time in months, he felt a spark of the passion that had once driven him.

Arjun continued to visit Rajan daily, and their conversations became the highlight of Rajan's day. The boy's innocence and enthusiasm were infectious. Slowly, Rajan began to see that his knowledge and experience still had value, even if he could no longer fly. He realized that he could still share his love of flying with others, that his life wasn't over—it had just taken a different direction.

The Road to Redemption

Inspired by his interactions with Arjun, Rajan began to take small steps towards rebuilding his life. He agreed to start physical therapy, not because he believed he would walk again, but because he wanted to regain some independence. The sessions were painful, both physically and emotionally, but Rajan persisted. With each small victory—learning to move his wheelchair on his own, being able to transfer from the bed to the chair—he felt a glimmer of hope.

Meanwhile, Rajan also began tutoring Arjun in math and science. The boy's interest in aviation grew, and Rajan found joy in teaching him everything he knew. Word spread, and soon other children from the village started coming to Rajan for lessons. What started as a way to pass the time became a new purpose in life. Rajan realized that he could inspire a new generation of pilots, engineers, and dreamers.

But Rajan's biggest challenge came when Arjun's father, a local school teacher, suggested that Rajan give a talk at the village school. The idea terrified him. He hadn't spoken in public since the accident, and he wasn't sure he could face a room full of people who had once known him as a confident, successful pilot. But Arjun's father insisted, reminding Rajan that his story could inspire others.

Rajan reluctantly agreed. On the day of the talk, he wheeled himself onto the stage, his heart pounding. The room was filled with students, teachers, and villagers—people who had once looked up to him. He started to speak, his voice shaky at first, but as he told his story—the thrill of flying, the horror of the crash, and the long road to recovery—he found his confidence returning. The audience was captivated, not just by the story of a man who had once flown planes, but by the story of a man who had learned to fly again in a different way.

The Legacy of Rajan Singh

The talk was a turning point for Rajan. It marked the beginning of a new chapter in his life, one where he was no longer defined by what he had lost, but by what he had gained—a new sense of purpose, a new way to contribute, and a new understanding of what it means to be resilient.

Rajan continued to teach and mentor children in the village, helping them with their studies and encouraging them to pursue their dreams. He also started an aviation club at the local school, where students could learn about planes, flight mechanics, and the principles of aerodynamics. Through his efforts, several of his students went on to pursue careers in aviation, fulfilling the dreams that Rajan could no longer achieve for himself.

But Rajan's greatest legacy was not in the number of pilots he trained or the students he inspired. It was in the lesson he imparted to everyone who knew him: that hope is not about what we can do, but about what we can be, even when life takes everything we thought we needed away from us. Rajan Singh showed that resilience is not about never falling, but about finding the strength to rise again, even when the odds seem insurmountable.

Conclusion

Rajan Singh's story is a testament to the enduring power of hope and the resilience of the human spirit. It is a reminder that even when life grounds us, we can find new ways to soar. Rajan's journey from despair to redemption teaches us that no matter how far we fall, there is always a way to rise again, to find purpose, and to make a difference. His life may have taken a path he never expected, but in the end, Rajan discovered that the true meaning of flight is not in the sky, but in the spirit that refuses to be grounded.

CHAPTER FIFTEEN

MANOJ DEY FROM SHADOWS OF SMALL TOWN TO THE SPOTLIGHT OF YOUTUBE

Introduction

In a world where success is often measured by fame and wealth, Manoj Dey's story stands out as a testament to the power of perseverance, resilience, and hope. From a small town in Jharkhand to becoming a well-known YouTuber with millions of followers, Manoj's journey is one of grit, determination, and an unwavering belief in the power of dreams. This chapter delves into the life of Manoj Dey—a man who rose from the shadows of obscurity to the spotlight of digital fame, inspiring countless others along the way.

Humble Beginnings

Manoj Dey was born and raised in the small town of Dhanbad, Jharkhand. Growing up in a modest family, Manoj's early life was marked by financial struggles. His father worked as a welder, earning just enough to make ends meet. Despite the hardships, Manoj was a curious and determined child, always eager to learn and explore new things. His parents, though limited in resources, did everything they could to support his education, understanding that knowledge was the key to a better future.

From a young age, Manoj was fascinated by technology. While his peers were content playing outdoor games, Manoj would spend hours tinkering with old radios, mobile phones, and anything else he could get his hands on. His love for technology, however, was often tempered by the harsh realities of life in a small town, where opportunities were scarce and dreams were often stifled by the need to survive.

The Struggles of a Young Dreamer

After completing his schooling, Manoj faced the daunting task of choosing a career path. His family's financial situation did not allow for the luxury of higher education, and Manoj found himself at a crossroads. He knew that pursuing a traditional job would help alleviate his family's financial burden, but his heart was set on something more—something that would allow him to combine his love for technology with his desire to make a difference.

It was around this time that Manoj discovered YouTube. Fascinated by the platform's potential to reach millions of people, he began dreaming of becoming a content creator. However, the path to becoming a YouTuber was far from easy. Manoj had no access to high-quality equipment, no formal training, and very little guidance. All he had was an old, second-hand smartphone and a borrowed laptop.

Undeterred by these limitations, Manoj decided to take the plunge. He started his first YouTube channel, creating videos on technology and mobile repairs—topics he was passionate about. His early videos were far from polished; the audio quality was poor, the visuals were shaky, and the editing was rudimentary. But Manoj's content was genuine, and his passion for sharing knowledge shone through.

Despite his best efforts, the initial response was disheartening. His videos struggled to gain views, and Manoj found himself questioning his decision. The harsh comments and lack of engagement from viewers were tough to handle, especially given the sacrifices he was making. But instead of giving up, Manoj saw each setback as a learning opportunity. He spent hours studying successful YouTubers, analyzing their content, and learning the intricacies of video production.

The Turning Point

The turning point in Manoj's YouTube journey came when he decided to focus on content that resonated with a broader audience. He realized that while there were many tech channels on YouTube, very few catered to the needs of viewers from rural areas who struggled with basic technological concepts. Manoj began creating videos that explained technology in simple, relatable terms, often using examples from everyday life.

This shift in focus proved to be a game-changer. Manoj's videos began to attract viewers from small towns and villages across India—people who found his content accessible and easy to understand. His subscriber count started to grow, and with it, his confidence. Manoj's channel began to stand out in a crowded space, not because of flashy production values, but because of the authenticity and relatability of his content.

As his channel grew, Manoj faced new challenges. The demands of content creation were relentless, and balancing his YouTube work with other responsibilities was difficult. Financially, he was still struggling, as the income from YouTube was not yet sufficient to support his family. There were times when Manoj considered giving up, but each time, he reminded himself of why he had started in the first place.

Rising Above the Odds

One of the most significant challenges Manoj faced was dealing with the expectations of those around him. His family and friends, while supportive, were skeptical of his decision to pursue YouTube full-time. In a small town like Dhanbad, the idea of making a living from YouTube was almost unheard of. Manoj often found himself defending his choices, explaining to others that YouTube was not just a hobby, but a legitimate career path.

The pressure was immense, but Manoj's determination was stronger. He continued to work tirelessly, producing content that was not only informative but also inspirational. He began sharing his own story—how he had started with nothing, how he had faced rejection and failure, and how he had persevered despite the odds. His honesty and openness resonated with his audience, many of whom were facing similar struggles in their own lives.

As Manoj's popularity grew, so did the opportunities. Brands began approaching him for collaborations, and his income from YouTube started to increase. But even as he tasted success, Manoj remained grounded. He knew that his journey was not just about making money or gaining fame; it was about using his platform to make a difference in the lives of others.

The Impact Beyond Numbers

Today, Manoj Dey is not just a successful YouTuber with millions of subscribers; he is a symbol of hope for countless young people who aspire to break free from the limitations imposed by their circumstances. Through his content, Manoj has inspired a generation of aspiring creators, showing them that with hard work, resilience, and a little bit of hope, they too can achieve their dreams.

Manoj's impact goes beyond the numbers on his YouTube channel. He regularly mentors young creators, sharing the lessons he has learned along the way. He has also used his platform to raise awareness about social issues, advocating for education, digital literacy, and the empowerment of rural communities. His story has been featured in various media outlets, and he has been invited to speak at events across the country, where he continues to inspire others with his journey.

But despite all his success, Manoj has never forgotten where he came from. He continues to live in Dhanbad, close to his family, and remains deeply connected to his roots. His story is a reminder that true success is not measured by wealth or fame, but by the impact one has on the lives of others.

Conclusion: A Legacy of Hope

Manoj Dey's journey from a small town in Jharkhand to becoming a YouTube sensation is a testament to the power of hope, determination, and resilience. It is a story that resonates with anyone who has ever faced adversity, anyone who has ever been told that their dreams are too big, and anyone who has ever doubted their own potential.

Through his life and work, Manoj has shown that no matter where you come from, no matter what challenges you face, you can achieve greatness if you are willing to work hard and never give up. His story is not just about one man's rise to fame; it is about the power of believing in yourself, even when the world doesn't.

As Manoj continues to create content, mentor young creators, and give back to his community, his legacy of hope will undoubtedly inspire generations to come. His journey is far from over, but one thing is certain: Manoj Dey is living proof that with hope and hard work, anything is possible.

UNSTOPPABLE

Chapter 16: Unstoppable: The Power of Persistence and Passion**
Introduction
Sandeep Maheshwari is a name that resonates with millions across India and beyond. His journey from a struggling photographer to one of the most successful entrepreneurs and motivational speakers is a testament to the power of persistence and passion. Among his many talks, the "Unstoppable" speech stands out as a powerful reminder that no matter what challenges life throws at us, we have the power to rise above them and become unstoppable.

This chapter delves into the essence of Sandeep Maheshwari's "Unstoppable" speech, breaking down its key messages and exploring the impact it has had on countless individuals striving to overcome their own obstacles.
The Beginning: A Life of Struggles
Sandeep begins his speech by acknowledging the universal nature of struggles. Everyone, regardless of their background, faces challenges in life. He candidly shares his own story—how he started his career as a photographer with little money, no guidance, and numerous failures along the way. Despite these hardships, he was driven by a burning desire to succeed, to prove to himself and to the world that he could achieve his dreams.

He emphasizes that struggles are not unique to any one person. Everyone faces difficulties, but what separates those who succeed from those who don't is how they respond to these challenges. According to Sandeep, it is this response—the willingness to keep going despite the odds—that makes a person unstoppable.

The Power of Belief

One of the central themes of Sandeep's speech is the power of belief. He urges his audience to believe in themselves and their abilities, even when no one else does. Sandeep shares how, during his early days, many people doubted his dreams. They questioned his choices and discouraged him from pursuing his passion. But instead of letting these doubts deter him, he used them as motivation to push harder.

"Belief is not about knowing the outcome," Sandeep says. "It's about having faith in the process. It's about trusting that, no matter what, you will find a way to make things work."

He emphasizes that belief is a choice. You can choose to believe in your dreams, in your ability to overcome obstacles, or you can choose to let fear and doubt control your life. The choice is yours, and it's a choice you must make every single day.

Taking Responsibility

Sandeep's speech also highlights the importance of taking responsibility for one's life. He believes that the moment you start blaming others—be it your circumstances, your upbringing, or other people—you lose control over your life. Taking responsibility means accepting where you are, recognizing that your current situation is a result of the choices you've made, and understanding that you have the power to change it.

"Don't wait for someone to come and rescue you," Sandeep urges. "Don't wait for the perfect opportunity. Start where you are, with what you have, and take responsibility for your life. Only then can you truly become unstoppable."

He explains that life is not always fair, and things will not always go as planned. However, how you respond to these situations is what defines your journey. By taking responsibility, you reclaim your power and position yourself as the creator of your own destiny.

Embracing Failure

Another key point in Sandeep's speech is the importance of embracing failure. He shares his personal experiences of failure—how he faced multiple setbacks, from failed business ventures to personal disappointments. But instead of viewing failure as a roadblock, Sandeep saw it as a stepping stone to success.

"Failure is not the opposite of success; it's a part of success," he says. "Every failure teaches you something valuable. It shows you what doesn't work, and brings you one step closer to what does."

Sandeep encourages his audience to redefine their relationship with failure. Rather than fearing it, they should welcome it as an essential part of the learning process. He emphasizes that those who are willing to fail, learn from their mistakes, and keep moving forward are the ones who ultimately succeed.

The Power of Persistence

Persistence is a recurring theme in Sandeep's speech. He believes that persistence—more than talent, intelligence, or luck—is the key to achieving greatness. He shares how, despite facing numerous rejections and setbacks, he never gave up on his dreams. It was this relentless persistence that eventually led him to success.

"Most people give up just when they're about to achieve success," Sandeep says. "They quit on the one-yard line. They give up at the last minute of the game, one foot from a winning touchdown. Don't be that person."

He stresses that persistence is not about blindly pushing forward; it's about adapting, learning, and continuously improving while staying committed to your goals. It's about the unwavering determination to keep moving, even when the road is rough and the future uncertain.

Passion: The Driving Force

For Sandeep, passion is the fuel that drives persistence. He talks about how passion gives you the energy to keep going, even when the odds are stacked against you. Passion is what makes the long hours, the sacrifices, and the setbacks worthwhile. Without passion, it's easy to lose motivation and give up when things get tough.

"Find what you're passionate about," Sandeep advises. "When you love what you do, work doesn't feel like work. It becomes a joy, a part of who you are. And when you're passionate about something, you'll find the strength to overcome any obstacle."

He encourages his audience to pursue their passions, no matter how unconventional or difficult they may seem. Passion, combined with persistence, is what makes a person truly unstoppable.

Living with Integrity

Sandeep's speech also touches on the importance of living with integrity. He believes that success without integrity is hollow. Integrity means being true to yourself, staying aligned with your values, and doing the right thing, even when it's difficult. For Sandeep, living with integrity is non-negotiable—it's the foundation upon which true success is built.

"Success that compromises your values is not real success," Sandeep asserts. "Stay true to who you are, and don't let the pursuit of success make you lose sight of what's important."

He reminds his audience that integrity is not just about big decisions; it's about the small, everyday choices that define who you are. It's about consistency, honesty, and staying grounded, no matter how high you rise.

Conclusion: Becoming Unstoppable

As Sandeep Maheshwari concludes his speech, he leaves his audience with a powerful message: "You are unstoppable." He reminds them that within each of us lies an incredible power—the power to dream, to persist, to overcome, and to achieve greatness. But to tap into that power, we must first believe in ourselves, take responsibility for our lives, embrace failure, and never give up.

"Success is not a destination; it's a journey," Sandeep says. "And that journey is made up of countless small steps, taken with courage, persistence, and passion. No matter where you are today, no matter what challenges you're facing, know this: You have the power to become unstoppable."

CHAPTER SEVENTEEN

KALPANA SAROJ

Kalpana Saroj: From Poverty to the Boardroom

Introduction: A Beacon of Resilience and Success

Kalpana Saroj's life is a remarkable tale of overcoming adversity through sheer determination, grit, and perseverance. Born into a Dalit family in rural Maharashtra, she faced the harsh realities of discrimination, poverty, and a life that seemed preordained for suffering. However, Kalpana refused to let her circumstances define her. From the brink of suicide to becoming one of India's most successful entrepreneurs, her journey exemplifies the power of belief in oneself and the ability to turn adversity into opportunity.

Her story is not just one of personal triumph, but also an inspiration to millions of women, marginalized individuals, and aspiring entrepreneurs. It's a reminder that with hope, resilience, and the will to fight back, one can rise from the lowest of lows to the highest peaks of success.

Early Life: The Weight of Poverty and Discrimination

Kalpana Saroj was born in 1961 into a Dalit family in the small village of Roperkheda, Maharashtra. Growing up, she faced the dual hardships of poverty and caste-based discrimination. As a Dalit, she and her family were considered "untouchable," living on the fringes of society, deprived of basic human dignity. From an early age, she understood that society had built invisible walls around people like her, walls she would eventually break down.

Her father worked as a police constable, earning a meager income that was barely enough to provide for the family. Despite their financial struggles, Kalpana's father valued education and made sure that his children, including Kalpana, attended school. But even in school, she faced discrimination. Her classmates from higher castes refused to sit next to her, and she was often ostracized because of her background.

The young Kalpana's resilience was evident even in her school years. Despite the humiliation and isolation she faced, she persevered in her studies, knowing that education was her only hope of escaping the shackles of poverty.

She watched her family struggle with finances, which instilled in her a deep desire to change her circumstances. Even at a young age, she believed that there had to be a way out, even if it wasn't clear yet.

At the age of 12, Kalpana's life took a devastating turn. Her family, under pressure from societal norms, married her off to a man in Mumbai. This child marriage would become a dark chapter in her life, one filled with misery, abuse, and despair.

Her husband's family treated her like a servant, and Kalpana was subjected to verbal and physical abuse on a daily basis. Her dreams of education and a better life seemed to fade away as she was confined to the oppressive environment of her in-laws' home. Isolated, young, and helpless, Kalpana endured unimaginable suffering. She could not understand why her life had become a nightmare.

For months, Kalpana lived in fear, completely cut off from her family and the outside world. The abuse she faced began to take a toll on her mentally and emotionally. At such a young age, the burden of this toxic relationship seemed unbearable.

The one thing that kept her going was her inner strength. Even in her darkest moments, she never let go of her desire to escape this life. She harbored a silent determination to find a way out.

At the age of 16, after years of abuse and neglect, Kalpana hit rock bottom. One day, when the weight of her misery became too much to bear, she made the decision to end her life. She consumed poison, believing that death was the only escape from her suffering. But fate had other plans for her.

Kalpana was rushed to a hospital where her life was saved. In the aftermath of the suicide attempt, something shifted inside her. Instead of being consumed by despair, she felt a newfound determination to live—not just live, but to thrive. She made a vow to herself that she would never let anyone else control her destiny again. She would take her life into her own hands.

This was the turning point in Kalpana's life. She decided that if she could survive the lowest moment of her life, she could survive anything. She returned to her father's home, determined to rebuild her life.

With the support of her father, she began to think about how she could turn her pain into purpose. She realized that she was responsible for creating her future.

The Beginning of a New Life: Finding Her Way in Mumbai

Kalpana returned to Mumbai, this time with a mission. She started working in a small tailoring shop, earning a modest wage. While it was far from glamorous, it was a start—a way to gain independence and learn the value of hard work. Kalpana knew that this was just the beginning, and she was willing to do whatever it took to rise above her circumstances.

Despite her limited education, Kalpana had a sharp business mind and an entrepreneurial spirit. She saved every rupee she earned, determined to invest in herself. Over the next few years, she worked multiple jobs, gaining experience and learning as much as she could about the business world.

First Small Venture: With her savings, Kalpana started a small tailoring business of her own. It was her first step toward financial independence, and she poured her heart into making it successful.

She took risks that others would shy away from, understanding that growth required courage. Every small victory was a step closer to her vision of a better life.

Kalpana also began to help people in her community, offering employment to women who were similarly marginalized. Even at this early stage of her journey, she understood the importance of lifting others up as she climbed.

Kalpana's big break came when she was approached to take over a bankrupt company—Kamani Tubes. The company, which was once a thriving manufacturer of copper tubes, had fallen into financial ruin due to mismanagement. Kamani Tubes was burdened with massive debt and labor unrest, and no one wanted to touch it. But Kalpana saw an opportunity where others saw a lost cause.

In 2000, she took the bold step of acquiring Kamani Tubes. It was a massive undertaking, and many people doubted her ability to turn the company around. After all, she had no formal education in business or management, and the company's situation seemed beyond salvage. But Kalpana had something more important than a business degree—she had vision, determination, and an unshakable belief in her ability to succeed.

Tackling Debt and Labor Issues: Kalpana's first task was to address the company's debt and labor disputes. She negotiated with banks and creditors, convincing them to restructure the company's loans. She also worked closely with the employees, building trust and ensuring that they were part of the company's revival.

Turning the Company Around: Slowly but surely, Kalpana turned Kamani Tubes into a profitable business once again. Through strategic decision-making, strong leadership, and a relentless work ethic, she breathed new life into the company.

Leadership by Example: Kalpana led by example, often working long hours and personally overseeing the company's operations. Her employees respected her because they saw how deeply invested she was in the company's success.

Kalpana's success as the head of Kamani Tubes marked the beginning of a new chapter in her life. She had proven that she could rise from the ashes of poverty and become a powerful force in the business world. But for Kalpana, her success was not just about personal wealth or recognition—it was about giving back and empowering others.

Throughout her career, she has been a vocal advocate for marginalized communities, particularly women and Dalits. She believes in the power of entrepreneurship as a tool for social change and has made it her mission to inspire others to pursue their dreams, no matter their background or circumstances.

Mentorship and Advocacy: Kalpana has mentored numerous young entrepreneurs, particularly women, helping them overcome the barriers that society often places in their way.

Championing Social Causes: She has also been involved in various social causes, from education and women's rights to supporting initiatives aimed at reducing poverty and improving health care in underprivileged communities.

The Power of Hope and Resilience: Lessons from Kalpana Saroj's Life

Kalpana Saroj's story is more than just a rags-to-riches tale. It's a story of hope, resilience, and the belief that one person, no matter how marginalized, can change the course of their life through determination and hard work. Her journey teaches us that:

Adversity is Not the End: No matter how difficult life gets, there is always a way forward. Kalpana's life was filled with unimaginable hardship, but she refused to let her circumstances dictate her future.

Failure is a Stepping Stone: Kalpana's early experiences with failure, including her first marriage and suicide attempt, did not define her. Instead, they became the catalyst for her eventual success.

Helping Others is the Greatest Success: Kalpana believes that true success lies in helping others succeed. Her commitment to empowering women and marginalized communities is a testament to the power of giving back.

Conclusion: A Legacy of Hope and Determination

Today, Kalpana Saroj is a symbol of hope and inspiration to millions of people across India and around the world. Her journey from the slums of Maharashtra to the boardrooms of corporate

India is a story of unparalleled courage and determination. It serves as a reminder that no matter where you start in life, you can rise above your circumstances and achieve greatness.

Kalpana Saroj's life is proof that resilience, hope, and hard work can turn even the most difficult circumstances into opportunities for growth and success. She continues to inspire a new generation of entrepreneurs and change-makers, showing them that with the right mindset, anything is possible.

PART 3

PART III

Practical Guidance

and

Interactive Content.

CHAPTER EIGHTEEN

REFLECTION AND SELF DISCOVERY

Reflection and Self-Discovery: The Journey Within**

Introduction: The Power of Looking Inward

In the hustle and bustle of modern life, it's easy to get caught up in external pursuits—career goals, relationships, societal expectations—while neglecting the internal landscape that shapes who we are. Yet, true growth and fulfillment come not just from achieving outward success but from understanding and nurturing our inner selves. Reflection and self-discovery are powerful tools that allow us to delve into the depths of our thoughts, emotions, and beliefs, helping us to uncover our true desires, strengths, and potential.

This chapter will explore the transformative power of reflection and self-discovery. Through a combination of introspective exercises, journaling prompts, and guided meditations, you will embark on a journey to better understand yourself and gain clarity on your life's path. Whether you're facing a significant life transition, seeking greater purpose, or simply wanting to deepen your self-awareness, this chapter is designed to help you connect with your inner self and unlock the answers that lie within.

The Importance of Self-Reflection

Self-reflection is the practice of intentionally examining your thoughts, feelings, and actions. It is a conscious effort to step back and observe your life from a distance, free from the distractions and noise of daily life. By reflecting on your experiences, you gain insights into your behaviors, motivations, and patterns, which in turn empowers you to make more informed decisions and live a more intentional life.

Why Reflect?

- **Clarity**: Self-reflection helps you clarify your values, goals, and desires. It allows you to sift through the clutter of your mind and focus on what truly matters.

- **Growth**: Reflection fosters personal growth by helping you learn from your experiences, both positive and negative. It turns mistakes into lessons and challenges into opportunities for development.

- **Self-Awareness**: Through reflection, you become more aware of your thoughts, emotions, and behaviors. This awareness is the first step toward self-improvement and emotional intelligence.

- **Alignment**: By regularly reflecting on your life, you can ensure that your actions and choices align with your core values and long-term goals.

How to Begin Reflecting

- **Set Aside Time**: Dedicate regular time to self-reflection. This could be daily, weekly, or monthly, depending on your schedule. The key is consistency.

- **Create a Quiet Space**: Find a quiet, comfortable space where you can reflect without interruptions. This could be a cozy corner of your home, a park bench, or even your car.

- **Ask the Right Questions**: Reflection is most effective when guided by thoughtful questions. Consider what you want to reflect on—your day, a specific event, or a recurring issue—and frame your reflections around these questions.

Guided Reflection Exercises

Reflection exercises are structured activities that help you explore specific aspects of your life. Below are several exercises designed to guide you through different facets of self-discovery.

1. Reflecting on Past Challenges

Challenges are inevitable in life, but they also provide valuable opportunities for growth. Reflecting on how you've navigated past challenges can reveal your strengths and areas for improvement.

- Exercise:

1. Choose a significant challenge you've faced in the past year.

2. Write a detailed account of the challenge, focusing on your thoughts, feelings, and actions during that time.

3. Reflect on the following questions:

- What was the hardest part of this challenge?

- How did you overcome it?

- What strengths did you draw upon?

- What did you learn about yourself through this experience?

- How has this challenge shaped who you are today?

- **Example**: Imagine you faced a difficult decision at work—whether to leave a stable job for a more fulfilling but uncertain opportunity. Reflecting on the experience might reveal that your decision-making process was heavily influenced by your fear of failure, but also by your desire for growth and personal satisfaction. Understanding this can help you approach future decisions with greater clarity.

2. Identifying Core Values

Your core values are the guiding principles that shape your decisions and behaviors. Understanding your values is crucial for living a life that feels authentic and fulfilling.

- Exercise:

1. Write down a list of values that are important to you (e.g., honesty, family, creativity, success, compassion).

2. Rank these values in order of importance, starting with the one that resonates most deeply with you.

3. Reflect on the following questions:

- How do these values manifest in your daily life?

- Are there any values on your list that you feel you're not honoring as much as you'd like?

- How can you align your actions more closely with your top values?

- *Example*: If "creativity" is one of your top values, but you find that you rarely engage in creative activities, this reflection might prompt you to make changes—such as setting aside time each week for a creative hobby or incorporating more creativity into your work.

3. The Wheel of Life

The Wheel of Life is a visual tool that helps you assess and balance different areas of your life. It provides a snapshot of where you are right now and identifies areas that may need more attention.

- Exercise:

1. Draw a circle and divide it into eight sections, like a pie. Label each section with a different area of your life (e.g., career, family, health, finances, personal growth, relationships, fun/recreation, spirituality).

2. On a scale of 1 to 10, rate your level of satisfaction in each area. 1 means you're completely dissatisfied, and 10 means you're fully satisfied.

3. Reflect on the following questions:

- Which areas of your life are thriving? Which are lacking?

- What steps can you take to improve the areas that scored lower?

- How can you maintain or further enhance the areas that scored higher?

- Example: If your "health" section scores low, you might reflect on your current lifestyle choices and decide to prioritize healthier habits, such as regular exercise or a balanced diet. If "personal growth" scores high, you might explore new ways to continue your development, such as enrolling in a course or setting new learning goals.

Journaling as a Tool for Self-Discovery

Journaling is one of the most effective ways to engage in self-reflection. It allows you to express your thoughts and emotions freely, track your progress over time, and explore different aspects of your identity. Journaling can be as structured or as free-flowing as you like, depending on what works best for you.

Types of Journaling
- **Free Writing**: Write continuously for a set period (e.g., 10 minutes), without worrying about grammar, punctuation, or coherence. The goal is to let your thoughts flow naturally.
- **Prompted Journaling**: Use specific prompts to guide your writing. Prompts can be questions, quotes, or statements that inspire reflection.
- **Gratitude Journaling**: Focus on writing about the things you're grateful for. This practice shifts your focus to the positive aspects of your life and fosters a sense of appreciation.

Journaling Prompts for Self-Discovery
- **What does success mean to me, and how has my definition of success changed over time?**
- **Describe a moment when you felt truly at peace. What were you doing, and what made that moment special?**
- **What are the top three lessons I've learned in life so far, and how have they shaped me?**
- **If I could go back and give my younger self one piece of advice, what would it be and why?**
- **What are the fears that hold me back from pursuing my dreams? How can I address these fears?**

Tips for Effective Journaling
- **Be Honest**: Your journal is a safe space where you can be completely honest with yourself. Don't censor your thoughts or emotions.
- **Consistency**: Try to journal regularly, whether it's daily, weekly, or whenever you feel the need to reflect. Consistency helps build the habit and deepens your self-discovery.
- **Revisit Your Entries**: Periodically review your past entries. This allows you to track your growth, identify patterns, and gain new insights.

Guided Meditation for Inner Clarity

Meditation is a powerful practice that complements self-reflection by helping you clear your mind, connect with your inner self, and gain clarity on your thoughts and emotions. Below is a simple guided meditation for inner clarity:

Preparation

- Find a quiet, comfortable place where you won't be disturbed.

- Sit in a comfortable position, with your back straight and your hands resting on your lap.

- Close your eyes and take a few deep breaths, inhaling through your nose and exhaling through your mouth.

Guided Meditation

1. **Focus on Your Breath**: Begin by focusing on your breath. Notice the sensation of the air entering your nostrils, filling your lungs, and then slowly leaving your body. Allow your breath to flow naturally, without trying to control it.

2. **Body Scan**: Gradually bring your awareness to different parts of your body, starting from the top of your head and moving down to your toes. Notice any areas of tension or discomfort, and with each exhale, imagine releasing that tension.

3. **Visualize a Place of Peace**: Imagine yourself in a place where you feel completely at peace. This could be a real place you feel completely at peace. This could be a real place you've been to or a place you create in your mind. It might be a serene beach, a quiet forest, or a cozy room. Spend a few moments visualizing the details of this place—what you see, hear, and feel.

Ask for Clarity: In your peaceful place, ask yourself a question that you seek clarity on. This could be something you're struggling with or a decision you need to make. Pose the question gently, without forcing an answer.

Listen to Your Inner Voice: After asking your question, simply sit in silence and listen. Don't try to analyze or rationalize. Just allow any thoughts, feelings, or images to arise naturally.

Return to Your Breath: When you feel ready, gradually bring your focus back to your breath. Take a few deep breaths, grounding yourself in the present moment.

Close the Meditation: Slowly open your eyes and take a moment to reorient yourself. Reflect on any insights or feelings that came up during the meditation.

Post-Meditation Reflection

After your meditation, consider journaling about your experience. What insights did you gain? How do you feel now compared to when you started?

Exploring Identity and Purpose

Self-discovery is deeply intertwined with the exploration of your identity and purpose. Understanding who you are—beyond the roles you play and the labels you carry—can lead to a more authentic and fulfilling life.

Exploring Identity Your identity is a complex tapestry woven from your beliefs, values, experiences, and relationships. It's the core of who you are, shaping how you see the world and your place in it.

Who Am I?: Reflect on the different aspects of your identity—cultural, social, personal. How do these aspects influence your choices and behaviors? Are there parts of your identity that you feel disconnected from or want to explore further?

Beyond Roles and Labels: Consider the roles and labels that define you—such as parent, partner, professional, student. While these are important, they don't encompass the entirety of who you are. Reflect on what lies beneath these roles. Who are you when all these labels are stripped away?

The Evolving Self: Remember that identity is not static. It evolves as you grow and change. Embrace this evolution and allow yourself to explore new aspects of your identity.

Discovering Purpose Purpose is the sense of meaning and direction in life. It's what gives your life a deeper significance and motivates you to pursue your goals.

What Drives Me?: Reflect on the things that inspire you and bring you joy. What activities make you lose track of time? What causes are you passionate about? These are often clues to your purpose.

Legacy and Impact: Consider the impact you want to have on the world. How do you want to be remembered? What difference do you want to make in the lives of others?

Living with Purpose: Once you've identified your purpose, think about how you can align your daily actions with it. Purpose doesn't have to be something grand or world-changing. It can be as simple as living in a way that brings you fulfillment and joy.

Challenges on the Path of Self-Discovery

The journey of self-discovery is not always easy. It can be challenging, uncomfortable, and even frightening at times. But it is also incredibly rewarding.

Facing the Unknown

Fear of Change: Self-discovery often leads to change, which can be scary. You may realize that certain aspects of your life no longer align with who you truly are. Embrace this fear as a sign of growth and trust that it will lead you to a more authentic life.

Confronting Shadows: As you explore your inner self, you may encounter parts of yourself that you've suppressed or ignored—your fears, insecurities, and past traumas. Facing these shadows is essential for healing and growth. Remember that these parts of you are not to be feared, but to be understood and integrated into your whole self.

Navigating Uncertainty

The Journey is Ongoing: Self-discovery is not a destination but a lifelong journey. There will be times when you feel lost or uncertain about who you are and where you're going. This is a natural part of the process. Trust that with time, clarity will come.

Seeking Support: Don't hesitate to seek support on your journey. Whether through therapy, counseling, or talking with trusted friends, having someone to guide and support you can make the process easier and more enriching.

Conclusion: Embracing the Journey

The journey of self-discovery is one of the most profound and rewarding endeavors you can undertake. It requires courage, honesty, and a willingness to explore the unknown. But as you delve deeper into your inner world, you will uncover truths that can transform your life, leading to greater self-awareness, fulfillment, and peace.

As you continue on this journey, remember that self-discovery is not about reaching a final destination or becoming a "perfect" version of yourself. It's about embracing who you are in all your complexity and continuing to grow, evolve, and align your life with your true self.

So take a deep breath, turn inward, and trust the process. The answers you seek are already within you, waiting to be discovered.

CHAPTER NINETEEN

GOAL SETTING AND PERSONAL GROWTH

Goal Setting and Personal Growth: Crafting Your Path to Success

Introduction: The Foundation of Personal Growth

Goal setting is a fundamental aspect of personal growth and success. It is the process of envisioning your desired outcomes and creating a structured plan to achieve them. Goals give your life direction, provide motivation, and help you measure your progress. However, setting goals is not just about achieving specific outcomes; it's about the journey of growth that occurs as you work towards them. This chapter delves into the art and science of goal setting, offering practical tools and strategies to help you achieve your dreams while fostering continuous personal development.

The Importance of Goal Setting

Setting goals is like drawing a map for your life. Without clear goals, it's easy to drift through life without purpose or direction. Goals provide you with a sense of purpose and a roadmap to follow, helping you stay focused on what truly matters.

Why Set Goals?

- **Clarity and Focus**: Goals help you clarify what you want in life. They allow you to focus your time and energy on the things that matter most, rather than getting distracted by less important tasks.

- **Motivation**: When you have clear goals, you have something to strive for. This creates motivation and a sense of urgency that propels you to take action.

- **Accountability**: Goals provide a benchmark for measuring your progress. They allow you to hold yourself accountable, ensuring that you stay on track.

- **Personal Growth**: The process of working towards your goals encourages personal development. It pushes you to step out of your comfort zone, learn new skills, and overcome challenges.

The Role of Goals in Personal Growth

Personal growth is the ongoing process of understanding and developing yourself in order to achieve your full potential. Goal setting plays a crucial role in this process by challenging you to stretch your abilities and achieve more than you thought possible. As you work towards your goals, you build self-discipline, resilience, and confidence, all of which contribute to your overall growth.

Types of Goals

Not all goals are created equal. To effectively set and achieve your goals, it's important to understand the different types of goals and how they fit into your life.

1. Short-Term Goals

Short-term goals are objectives that you aim to achieve in the near future—typically within a few days, weeks, or months. These goals are often more specific and easier to accomplish, making them ideal for building momentum and confidence.

- **Examples**:
- Completing a work project by the end of the week.
- Starting a daily exercise routine.
- Reading a book on personal development within the next month.

2. Long-Term Goals

Long-term goals are objectives that require a longer time frame to achieve—typically several months, years, or even decades. These goals often represent major life aspirations, such as career success, financial independence, or personal fulfillment.
- **Examples**:
- Earning a degree or professional certification.
- Saving for retirement or purchasing a home.
- Building a successful business or writing a book.
3. Outcome Goals vs. Process Goals
- **Outcome Goals**: These are goals that focus on a specific result or achievement. For example, "losing 20 pounds" or "getting a promotion" are outcome goals. They are typically easier to measure but can be influenced by factors outside your control.
- **Process Goals**: These are goals that focus on the actions and behaviors that will lead to the desired outcome. For example, "exercising five times a week" or "applying for three new jobs each month" are process goals. These goals are entirely within your control and often lead to more sustainable progress.
4. Personal vs. Professional Goals
- **Personal Goals**: These goals relate to your personal life and well-being, including your health, relationships, hobbies, and personal development.
- **Professional Goals**: These goals are related to your career, such as achieving a promotion, improving your skills, or expanding your professional network.
Understanding these different types of goals allows you to set a balanced mix that aligns with your overall vision for your life.
The SMART Goals Framework
One of the most effective methods for setting goals is the SMART framework. SMART stands for Specific, Measurable, Achievable, Relevant, and Time-bound. This framework helps you create clear, actionable goals that are more likely to be achieved.
1. Specific
A specific goal is clear and unambiguous. It answers the questions of who, what, where, when, and why. The more specific

your goal, the easier it is to understand what you need to do to achieve it.

- **Example**: Instead of setting a vague goal like "get fit," set a specific goal like "lose 10 pounds by running three times a week and eating a balanced diet."

2. Measurable

A measurable goal has criteria that allow you to track your progress and determine when you have achieved it. It includes quantifiable elements, such as numbers, deadlines, or milestones.

- **Example**: "Save $5,000 in the next six months" is a measurable goal because you can track how much you've saved each month and know when you've reached your target.

3. Achievable

An achievable goal is realistic and attainable given your current resources, skills, and time frame. It should challenge you, but it should also be within your capabilities.

- **Example**: If you've never run a marathon before, setting a goal to run a 5K race within three months is more achievable than aiming to run a marathon within the same time frame.

4. Relevant

A relevant goal aligns with your broader life objectives and values. It should matter to you and contribute to your overall growth and well-being.

- **Example**: If your long-term goal is to improve your health, setting a goal to quit smoking is relevant, as it directly impacts your overall health and well-being.

5. Time-bound

A time-bound goal has a specific deadline or time frame for completion. This creates a sense of urgency and helps you prioritize your actions.

- **Example**: "Complete my thesis by the end of the semester" is a time-bound goal, as it has a clear deadline.

Creating Your SMART Goals

- **Step 1**: Choose a specific area of your life where you want to set a goal.

- **Step 2**: Write down your goal, making sure it meets all the SMART criteria.

- **Step 3**: Break down your goal into smaller, actionable steps.

- **Step 4**: Set deadlines for each step and track your progress regularly.

- **Step 5**: Adjust your plan as needed based on your progress and any changes in your circumstances.

Strategies for Achieving Your Goals

Setting goals is only the first step; achieving them requires consistent action and dedication. Here are some strategies to help you stay on track and achieve your goals.

1. Break Down Your Goals into Smaller Steps

Large goals can feel overwhelming, making it difficult to know where to start. By breaking down your goals into smaller, manageable steps, you can make steady progress without feeling overwhelmed.

- **Example**: If your goal is to write a book, start by setting smaller goals such as "write 500 words a day" or "complete one chapter per month."

2. Create a Vision Board

A vision board is a visual representation of your goals and dreams. It serves as a powerful reminder of what you're working towards and helps keep you motivated.

- **How to Create a Vision Board**:

- Gather images, quotes, and words that represent your goals and aspirations.

- Arrange them on a board, collage, or digital platform in a way that inspires you.

- Place your vision board somewhere you'll see it daily, such as your bedroom or workspace.

3. Use the 80/20 Rule

The 80/20 Rule, also known as the Pareto Principle, suggests that 80% of your results come from 20% of your efforts. Focus on the activities that have the most significant impact on achieving your goals, and minimize or eliminate tasks that don't contribute much value.

- **Example**: If your goal is to improve your sales at work, focus on the 20% of clients or strategies that generate 80% of your revenue.

4. Stay Accountable

Accountability is crucial for staying on track with your goals. Share your goals with a trusted friend, mentor, or accountability partner who can support you, provide feedback, and hold you accountable.

- **How to Stay Accountable**:

- Set regular check-ins with your accountability partner to review your progress.

- Join a support group or community of like-minded individuals who share similar goals.

- Use accountability apps or tools to track your progress and set reminders.

5. Celebrate Your Successes

It's important to celebrate your achievements, no matter how small they may seem. Celebrating your successes reinforces positive behavior and motivates you to continue working towards your goals.

- **Ways to Celebrate**:

- Reward yourself with something special, such as a treat, a day off, or a small gift.

- Reflect on your progress and express gratitude for the steps you've taken.

- Share your success with others and allow them to celebrate with you.

6. Learn from Setbacks

Setbacks are a natural part of the goal-setting process. Instead of viewing them as failures, see them as opportunities to learn and grow. Reflect on what went wrong, adjust your approach, and continue moving forward.

Steps to Overcome Setbacks:

Identify the cause of the setback and what you can learn from it.

Adjust your goals or action plan if necessary.

Stay resilient and keep your focus on the long-term goal.

Goal Setting as a Pathway to Personal Growth

As you work towards your goals, you'll notice that the process itself contributes significantly to your personal growth. Here's how goal setting can lead to continuous development:

1. Building Self-Discipline Achieving goals requires self-discipline—the ability to stay focused, avoid distractions, and stick to your plan even when motivation wanes. By consistently working towards your goals, you strengthen your self-discipline, which benefits all areas of your life.

2. Developing Resilience The journey to achieving your goals will inevitably include challenges and setbacks. Overcoming these obstacles builds resilience—the ability to bounce back from adversity and keep moving forward. Resilience is a key trait for personal growth, helping you navigate life's ups and downs with confidence.

3. Enhancing Time Management Effective goal setting requires good time management skills. As you juggle different tasks and priorities, you learn how to manage your time efficiently, ensuring that you make steady progress towards your goals without becoming overwhelmed.

4. Boosting Self-Confidence Each time you achieve a goal, no matter how small, you boost your self-confidence. This growing confidence encourages you to set and achieve even more ambitious goals, creating a positive cycle of growth and achievement.

5. Expanding Your Comfort Zone Goal setting often involves stepping out of your comfort zone and trying new things. This expansion of your comfort zone helps you grow as a person, exposing you to new experiences, skills, and perspectives.

6. Gaining a Sense of Purpose Working towards meaningful goals gives your life direction and purpose. It helps you connect with your deeper values and aspirations, providing a sense of fulfillment and satisfaction.

Overcoming Common Challenges in Goal Setting

Despite your best intentions, you may encounter obstacles that make it difficult to achieve your goals. Here are some common challenges and strategies to overcome them:

1. Procrastination Procrastination is one of the biggest barriers to goal achievement. It's easy to put off tasks, especially when they seem daunting or uncomfortable.

Solution: Break tasks down into smaller steps, set deadlines, and use techniques like the Pomodoro Technique (working in short, focused intervals) to stay on track.

2. Lack of Motivation Motivation can fluctuate, making it hard to stay committed to your goals over the long term.

Solution: Reconnect with the "why" behind your goals. Remind yourself of the benefits and rewards that achieving your goals will bring. Surround yourself with supportive people who can help keep you motivated.

3. Overwhelm Setting too many goals or tackling goals that are too ambitious can lead to overwhelm, making it difficult to make progress.

Solution: Prioritize your goals and focus on one or two key objectives at a time. Break down large goals into smaller, manageable tasks, and celebrate small wins along the way.

4. Fear of Failure Fear of failure can paralyze you, preventing you from taking action or pursuing your goals.

Solution: Embrace failure as a learning opportunity. Shift your mindset from fearing failure to viewing it as a necessary part of the growth process. Remember that every successful person has experienced setbacks along the way.

5. Lack of Resources Sometimes, you may feel that you lack the resources—time, money, skills, or support—needed to achieve your goals.

Solution: Be resourceful and creative. Seek out alternative solutions, such as free or low-cost resources, online courses, or community support. Break down your goals into smaller steps that you can achieve with the resources you have available.

Creating a Personal Growth Plan

To fully harness the power of goal setting for personal growth, consider creating a Personal Growth Plan—a structured roadmap that outlines your goals, action steps, and strategies for continuous development.

Steps to Create Your Personal Growth Plan

Define Your Vision: Start by defining your long-term vision for your life. What do you want to achieve in the next 5, 10, or 20 years? What kind of person do you want to become?

Identify Your Goals: Based on your vision, identify specific goals that align with your long-term aspirations. These should include a mix of short-term, long-term, personal, and professional goals.

Create an Action Plan: For each goal, outline the specific steps you need to take to achieve it. Include deadlines, milestones, and resources needed.

Set Up a Review Process: Regularly review your progress towards your goals. Adjust your plan as needed based on your progress and any changes in your circumstances.

Commit to Continuous Learning: Personal growth is an ongoing process. Commit to continuous learning and self-improvement by seeking out new opportunities for development, such as courses, books, workshops, or mentorship.

Example of a Personal Growth Plan

Vision: In 10 years, I want to be a successful entrepreneur, leading a business that positively impacts the environment, while also maintaining a healthy work-life balance.

Goal 1 (Short-Term): Complete a course in sustainable business practices within the next six months.

Goal 2 (Long-Term): Launch a sustainable business within the next three years.

Goal 3 (Personal): Improve my physical health by exercising at least four times a week.

Action Steps for Goal 1:

Research and enroll in an online course on sustainable business practices by [specific date].

Allocate two hours every evening to study and complete course assignments.

Apply the knowledge gained in a small project or case study.

Commitment to Growth: Review my Personal Growth Plan every quarter, update my goals and action steps as needed, and seek out new learning opportunities that align with my vision.

Conclusion: The Journey of Goal Setting and Personal Growth

Goal setting is not just about achieving specific outcomes; it's about the person you become in the process. By setting and working towards meaningful goals, you create a life that is purposeful, fulfilling, and constantly evolving. Each goal you achieve brings you closer to your full potential, while each challenge you overcome strengthens your resilience and character.

As you continue on your journey of personal growth, remember that the most important part is not the destination but the growth and learning that occurs along the way. Embrace the process, celebrate your progress, and stay committed to becoming the best version of yourself. With clear goals, consistent action, and a growth-oriented mindset, you have the power to create the life you've always dreamed of.

CHAPTER TWENTY

CULTIVATING A RESILLIENT MINDSET

Cultivating a Resilient Mindset: The Strength to Rise Above

Introduction: The Essence of Resilience

Life is filled with challenges, setbacks, and unexpected twists. While these obstacles can sometimes feel overwhelming, they also present opportunities for growth and learning. The key to navigating these difficulties lies in cultivating a resilient mindset—a mental and emotional strength that allows you to bounce back from adversity and continue moving forward. Resilience is not just about surviving tough times; it's about thriving despite them, using each experience to become stronger and wiser.

In this chapter, we will explore the concept of resilience, its importance in personal and professional life, and practical strategies for developing and sustaining a resilient mindset.

Understanding Resilience

Resilience is the capacity to recover quickly from difficulties and adapt well in the face of adversity, trauma, tragedy, or significant stress. It's the mental toughness that helps you cope with challenges and emerge from them stronger than before.

Key Characteristics of Resilient Individuals

Emotional Regulation: Resilient people can manage their emotions effectively, even in stressful situations. They don't let fear, anger, or frustration dictate their actions.

Optimism: Resilient individuals maintain a positive outlook, even when faced with difficulties. They focus on what they can control and believe that things will eventually improve.

Problem-Solving Skills: Resilient people approach challenges with a solution-oriented mindset. They view problems as opportunities to find creative solutions rather than insurmountable barriers.

Flexibility: Resilient individuals are adaptable and open to change. They can adjust their strategies and approaches when circumstances shift, without losing sight of their goals.

Self-Compassion: Resilient people are kind to themselves. They understand that setbacks are a natural part of life and treat themselves with the same compassion they would offer a friend.

The Importance of Resilience Resilience is essential for both personal and professional success. It enables you to handle stress, overcome obstacles, and pursue your goals despite the inevitable challenges. Resilience is also closely linked to mental health, as it helps you cope with stress and reduce the risk of anxiety and depression.

In the workplace, resilience is increasingly recognized as a critical skill. It allows you to navigate the pressures of deadlines, adapt to changing job roles, and bounce back from failures. In personal life, resilience helps you maintain relationships, manage health issues, and recover from losses.

The Science of Resilience

Research in psychology and neuroscience has shown that resilience is not a fixed trait but a dynamic process that can be developed and strengthened over time. The brain's neuroplasticity—its ability to change and adapt—plays a key role in building resilience.

Neuroplasticity and Resilience Neuroplasticity refers to the brain's ability to reorganize itself by forming new neural connections throughout life. This ability allows the brain to adapt to new experiences, learn new skills, and recover from injuries. When you practice resilient behaviors, such as positive thinking, problem-solving, and stress management, you strengthen the neural pathways associated with these behaviors. Over time, these pathways become more robust, making resilience a more natural and automatic response.

The Role of Hormones and Neurotransmitters Certain hormones and neurotransmitters also play a role in resilience. For example, cortisol, the "stress hormone," is released in response to stress. While cortisol is essential for the "fight or flight" response, chronic stress can lead to elevated cortisol levels, which can harm your health and well-being. Resilient individuals tend to have a more balanced stress response, with lower baseline cortisol levels and quicker recovery after a stressful event.

Endorphins, dopamine, and serotonin—often referred to as "feel-good" neurotransmitters—are also linked to resilience. Activities that increase these neurotransmitters, such as exercise, social interaction, and positive thinking, can boost your resilience by enhancing your mood and overall sense of well-being.

Building a Resilient Mindset

Cultivating a resilient mindset involves developing habits and attitudes that help you cope with challenges and bounce back from setbacks. Here are some strategies to help you build resilience:

1. Embrace a Growth Mindset A growth mindset is the belief that your abilities and intelligence can be developed through effort, learning, and perseverance. This mindset contrasts with a fixed mindset, where you believe that your talents and abilities are static and unchangeable.

How to Develop a Growth Mindset:

View Challenges as Opportunities: Instead of avoiding challenges, see them as opportunities to learn and grow. Embrace the process of trial and error, and understand that mistakes are a natural part of learning.

Focus on Effort, Not Just Results: Celebrate the effort you put into achieving your goals, rather than just the outcomes. This shift in focus encourages persistence, even when results aren't immediate.

Learn from Criticism: Use constructive criticism as a tool for growth. Rather than taking it personally, view it as valuable feedback that can help you improve.

2. Practice Emotional Regulation Emotional regulation is the ability to manage and respond to your emotions in a healthy and constructive way. Resilient individuals can remain calm under pressure and avoid being overwhelmed by negative emotions.

Techniques for Emotional Regulation:

Mindfulness Meditation: Practicing mindfulness helps you stay present and observe your emotions without judgment. This awareness allows you to respond to emotions rather than react impulsively.

Breathing Exercises: Deep breathing techniques, such as diaphragmatic breathing, can help calm your nervous system and reduce stress.

Cognitive Reframing: Reframing involves changing the way you perceive a situation. By viewing a challenge as a learning opportunity rather than a threat, you can shift your emotional response to a more positive and productive one.

3. Cultivate Optimism Optimism is the tendency to focus on the positive aspects of a situation and expect good outcomes. While some people are naturally more optimistic, optimism can be cultivated through practice.

Ways to Cultivate Optimism:

Practice Gratitude: Regularly reflecting on the things you're grateful for can shift your focus from what's going wrong to what's going right in your life.

Challenge Negative Thoughts: When negative thoughts arise, challenge them by considering alternative perspectives. Ask yourself, "Is there another way to look at this situation?" or "What's the silver lining?"

Surround Yourself with Positivity: Spend time with positive, supportive people who encourage and uplift you. Avoid negative influences that drain your energy and optimism.

4. Strengthen Your Problem-Solving Skills Problem-solving is a critical component of resilience. Resilient individuals approach challenges with a solution-oriented mindset, focusing on what they can do to overcome the obstacle rather than dwelling on the problem itself.

Steps to Improve Problem-Solving:

Define the Problem Clearly: Break down the problem into specific, manageable components. Understand what's causing the issue and identify the key factors involved.

Brainstorm Solutions: Generate a list of possible solutions, considering both conventional and creative approaches. Don't dismiss any ideas at this stage; instead, explore all possibilities.

Evaluate and Implement: Assess the potential outcomes of each solution and choose the one that seems most effective. Take action, and be prepared to adjust your approach if necessary.

5. Develop Strong Social Connections Resilience is not just an individual trait; it's also influenced by your relationships and social support networks. Strong social connections provide emotional support, practical help, and a sense of belonging, all of which contribute to resilience.

Building and Maintaining Relationships:

Nurture Existing Relationships: Invest time and effort into maintaining your current relationships. Regularly check in with friends and family, offer support when needed, and show appreciation for their presence in your life.

Seek Out New Connections: Don't be afraid to reach out and form new relationships. Join groups, clubs, or communities that align with your interests, and be open to meeting new people.

Practice Active Listening: When interacting with others, focus on truly listening to their concerns and experiences. This fosters deeper connections and strengthens your support network.

Daily Practices to Foster Resilience

Building resilience is an ongoing process that requires consistent effort. Incorporating the following daily practices into your routine can help you strengthen and maintain a resilient mindset:

1. Mindfulness and Meditation Mindfulness is the practice of being fully present in the moment, without judgment. It helps you stay grounded, manage stress, and cultivate a more balanced perspective.

Daily Mindfulness Practice:

Start Small: Begin with just a few minutes of mindfulness each day, gradually increasing the duration as you become more comfortable with the practice.

Use Guided Meditations: Guided meditations can help you stay focused and provide structure for your mindfulness practice. There are many apps and online resources available to get you started.

Incorporate Mindfulness into Daily Activities: Practice mindfulness during everyday tasks, such as eating, walking, or brushing your teeth. Focus on the sensations, sounds, and movements associated with each activity.

2. Gratitude Journaling Gratitude journaling is a simple yet powerful practice that shifts your focus from what's lacking to what's abundant in your life. It enhances your overall well-being and fosters a more positive outlook.

How to Keep a Gratitude Journal:

Set Aside Time: Dedicate a few minutes each day, either in the morning or before bed, to write down three to five things you're grateful for.

Be Specific: Instead of general statements like "I'm grateful for my family," be specific about what you appreciate, such as "I'm grateful for the laughter I shared with my family at dinner tonight."

Reflect on Your Entries: Periodically review your journal entries to remind yourself of the positive aspects of your life, especially during challenging times.

3. Positive Affirmations Positive affirmations are statements that you repeat to yourself to reinforce positive beliefs and attitudes. They help you build confidence, reduce stress, and maintain a

resilient mindset.

Creating and Using Affirmations:

Identify Areas for Growth: Consider areas of your life where you want to build resilience or confidence. Create affirmations that address these areas, such as "I am capable of overcoming any challenge" or "I embrace change with an open mind."

Repeat Regularly: Repeat your affirmations daily, either aloud or silently. Incorporate them into your morning routine or use them as a mental boost throughout the day.

Visualize Success: As you repeat your affirmations, visualize yourself embodying the qualities you're affirming. This reinforces the positive beliefs and helps you internalize them.

4. Physical Exercise Regular physical exercise is not only beneficial for your body but also for your mind. Exercise releases endorphins, which reduce stress and improve mood, making it an effective tool for building resilience.

Incorporating Exercise into Your Routine:

Find Activities You Enjoy: Choose physical activities that you enjoy, whether it's running, yoga, dancing, or playing a sport. This increases the likelihood that you'll stick with it.

Set Realistic Goals: Start with manageable fitness goals and gradually increase the intensity or duration of your workouts. Consistency is more important than intensity.

Combine Physical and Mental Benefits: Consider activities that combine physical exercise with mental relaxation, such as yoga or tai chi. These practices enhance both physical fitness and mental resilience.

5. Adequate Rest and Recovery Rest and recovery are essential components of resilience. Without adequate rest, both your mind and body become fatigued, making it harder to cope with stress and challenges.

Prioritizing Sleep:

Establish a Sleep Routine: Go to bed and wake up at the same time each day, even on weekends. This helps regulate your body's internal clock and improves the quality of your sleep.

Create a Relaxing Bedtime Ritual: Engage in calming activities before bed, such as reading, meditating, or taking a warm bath. Avoid screens and stimulating activities that can interfere with sleep.

Optimize Your Sleep Environment: Make your bedroom conducive to sleep by keeping it cool, dark, and quiet. Invest in a comfortable mattress and pillows that support restful sleep.

Resilience in Action: Overcoming Real-Life Challenges

Building resilience is not just about preparing for future challenges; it's about applying these principles in your daily life. Here are some real-life examples of how resilience can help you navigate common challenges:

1. Career Setbacks Imagine you've been working hard for a promotion, only to find out that the position has been given to someone else. This setback could easily lead to frustration, disappointment, or self-doubt. However, a resilient mindset would help you view this situation differently.

Resilient Response:

Reframe the Situation: Instead of seeing the setback as a failure, view it as an opportunity to learn and grow. Ask for feedback on why you weren't selected and use this information to improve your skills.

Stay Positive and Persistent: Maintain a positive attitude and continue to work towards your career goals. Recognize that setbacks are temporary and that your efforts will eventually pay off.

2. Relationship Challenges Relationships, whether with family, friends, or partners, can be a source of joy and support, but they can also present challenges. Misunderstandings, conflicts, and changes in life circumstances can strain even the strongest relationships.

Resilient Response:

Communicate Openly: Address issues directly and honestly with the other person involved. Effective communication is key to resolving conflicts and strengthening relationships.

Practice Forgiveness: Let go of grudges and resentment, which can weigh you down emotionally. Forgiving others—and yourself—frees you to move forward with a lighter heart.

Focus on Solutions, Not Problems: Instead of dwelling on what went wrong, focus on finding solutions that work for both parties. This solution-oriented approach helps rebuild trust and connection.

3. Personal Health Issues Health challenges, whether physical or mental, can be particularly difficult to navigate. They often require a great deal of resilience to cope with the uncertainty, pain, and lifestyle changes that come with them.

Resilient Response:

Seek Support: Don't hesitate to reach out to healthcare professionals, support groups, or loved ones for help. Building a support network is crucial for managing health challenges.

Maintain a Positive Outlook: Focus on what you can do to improve your health and well-being, rather than what's beyond your control. Set realistic goals for recovery and celebrate small victories.

Stay Informed and Proactive: Educate yourself about your condition and take an active role in your treatment plan. Being proactive gives you a sense of control and empowers you to make informed decisions.

Conclusion: Resilience as a Lifelong Practice

Resilience is not a trait you either have or don't have; it's a skill that you can develop and strengthen over time. By cultivating a resilient mindset, you equip yourself to handle life's challenges with grace and determination, emerging from each experience stronger and more capable than before.

As you continue on your journey of personal growth, remember that resilience is not about avoiding difficulties—it's about embracing them as opportunities for growth. By practicing the strategies outlined in this chapter and integrating them into your daily life, you can build a foundation of resilience that will support you through whatever life throws your way.

The path to resilience is ongoing, but with each step, you move closer to becoming the person you aspire to be—one who can face adversity with courage, overcome obstacles with determination, and thrive in the face of challenges. Embrace the journey, and know that every setback is a chance to build the strength and resilience you need to achieve your fullest potential.

CHAPTER TWENTY-ONE

COMMUNITY AND CONNECTION

Community and Connection: The Power of Belonging

Introduction: The Human Need for Connection

Humans are inherently social beings, wired for connection. From the moment we are born, we seek bonds with others—for comfort, for support, and for survival. This need for connection doesn't diminish as we grow older; if anything, it becomes more complex and essential. Whether through family, friendships, or larger communities, these connections play a crucial role in our overall well-being and personal growth.

In today's fast-paced, increasingly digital world, it's easy to overlook the importance of genuine, face-to-face connections. However, the value of community and connection cannot be overstated. They provide us with a sense of belonging, support us through life's challenges, and enrich our lives with shared experiences and collective wisdom. This chapter explores the significance of community and connection, offering insights into why they matter and how to cultivate them in your own life.

The Importance of Community and Connection

1. Emotional Support and Well-being One of the most significant benefits of strong social connections is the emotional support they provide. When life becomes challenging, having people you can turn to—whether for advice, comfort, or just a listening ear—makes

a world of difference.

Emotional Buffer: Social connections act as a buffer against stress, reducing its impact on your mental and emotional health. They provide reassurance and a sense of security, reminding you that you're not alone in your struggles.

Happiness and Fulfillment: Studies have consistently shown that people with strong social networks are happier, healthier, and live longer than those who are isolated. Meaningful relationships contribute to a sense of fulfillment and purpose in life.

2. Personal Growth and Development Connections with others are a vital component of personal growth. Through interactions with different people, you gain new perspectives, learn from their experiences, and expand your understanding of the world.

Learning from Others: Engaging with a diverse range of individuals exposes you to different ideas, cultures, and viewpoints. This diversity enriches your life and helps you develop empathy, critical thinking, and adaptability.

Accountability and Motivation: Being part of a community often means having others who hold you accountable to your goals and aspirations. Their encouragement and feedback can motivate you to push beyond your limits and achieve more than you might on your own.

3. A Sense of Belonging Belonging is a fundamental human need. Being part of a community where you feel accepted and valued contributes to your self-esteem and overall sense of identity.

Identity and Purpose: Your connections and community help shape your identity. They provide a sense of continuity and shared purpose, grounding you in a collective that gives meaning to your life.

Collective Strength: In times of crisis or change, communities offer collective strength. The shared resources, knowledge, and emotional support within a community make it easier to navigate difficult times.

4. Contribution and Impact Being part of a community isn't just about what you gain; it's also about what you contribute.

Contributing to the well-being of others provides a sense of purpose and fulfillment.

Giving Back: Acts of kindness, volunteering, and helping others in your community can boost your self-worth and reinforce your connections with those around you. Knowing that you're making a positive difference in someone's life enhances your own sense of purpose.

Building a Legacy: Through your contributions, you help build and sustain a community that can benefit future generations. This legacy of connection and support can have a lasting impact long after your direct involvement.

Building and Maintaining Meaningful Relationships

Meaningful relationships don't happen by accident; they require effort, intention, and mutual respect. Whether you're looking to deepen existing relationships or build new ones, the following strategies can help you cultivate strong, lasting connections.

1. Cultivate Genuine Interest in Others Strong relationships are built on mutual understanding and interest. Taking the time to learn about the people in your life—what they value, what they're passionate about, and what challenges they face—strengthens your bond.

Active Listening: Practice active listening by giving others your full attention when they speak. Avoid interrupting, and instead, ask open-ended questions that encourage them to share more. Listening deeply to someone shows that you value their thoughts and feelings.

Empathy: Put yourself in the other person's shoes. Try to understand their emotions and perspectives, even if they differ from your own. Empathy is key to building trust and creating a supportive environment.

Shared Experiences: Seek out opportunities to share experiences with others, whether through hobbies, travel, or volunteer work. These shared moments create lasting memories and deepen your connection.

2. Be Open and Vulnerable Vulnerability is the foundation of strong relationships. It allows others to see your authentic self, which in turn fosters trust and intimacy.

Share Your Stories: Don't be afraid to share your personal stories, struggles, and dreams with others. When you open up, you invite others to do the same, creating a space for genuine connection.

Express Your Needs: Healthy relationships involve mutual support. Don't hesitate to express your needs or ask for help when you need it. Allowing others to support you strengthens the bond between you.

Accept Imperfections: Recognize that no one is perfect, including yourself. Accepting and embracing each other's flaws and imperfections is a vital part of maintaining a strong, lasting relationship.

3. Invest Time and Energy Building and maintaining relationships requires time and effort. Prioritize your relationships by making time for the people who matter to you.

Regular Check-ins: Make it a habit to regularly check in with friends, family, and colleagues. A simple message or call to ask how they're doing can go a long way in maintaining the connection.

Quality Time: When spending time with others, focus on quality rather than quantity. Engage in meaningful conversations, plan activities you both enjoy, and be fully present in the moment.

Consistency: Consistency is key to maintaining relationships. Whether it's meeting up regularly, celebrating milestones together, or simply staying in touch, consistent effort keeps the connection strong.

4. Resolve Conflicts with Care Conflict is a natural part of any relationship, but how you handle it can make or break the connection. Approaching conflicts with care and understanding helps preserve and strengthen your relationships.

Communicate Openly: Address issues directly and respectfully. Use "I" statements to express how you feel, rather than blaming or accusing the other person. For example, say "I felt hurt when..."

instead of "You always..."

Seek to Understand: Before reacting, take the time to understand the other person's perspective. Ask clarifying questions and listen without interrupting. Understanding their point of view helps you respond more thoughtfully.

Find Common Ground: Look for areas of agreement or compromise. Focus on finding solutions that satisfy both parties, rather than winning the argument. Remember, the goal is to strengthen the relationship, not to "win."

5. Give and Receive Support Mutual support is a cornerstone of strong relationships. Being there for others when they need help—and allowing them to support you in return—deepens trust and connection.

Offer Help Freely: Whether it's lending a hand during a difficult time, offering a listening ear, or simply being present, small acts of support can have a significant impact. Offer help without expecting anything in return.

Be Gracious in Receiving Support: Accepting help from others isn't a sign of weakness; it's a recognition of the value of your relationships. Allow others the opportunity to support you, and express gratitude for their kindness.

Creating and Nurturing Community

Community extends beyond individual relationships. It encompasses the broader network of connections that bind people together, whether in a neighborhood, workplace, or interest-based group. Creating and nurturing a sense of community is essential for fostering belonging, collaboration, and collective well-being.

1. Identify Your Communities The first step in nurturing a sense of community is identifying the groups you are or wish to be a part of. These could be based on geography, shared interests, professional affiliations, or cultural connections.

Local Communities: Your neighborhood or town is a natural community. Getting involved in local events, supporting local businesses, and participating in community projects helps strengthen these ties.

Interest-Based Communities: Whether it's a hobby, sport, or cause you're passionate about, interest-based communities offer a space to connect with like-minded individuals. Joining clubs, groups, or online forums related to your interests can expand your social network.

Professional Communities: Networking within your industry or profession helps you build relationships that can support your career growth. Attend conferences, join professional associations, and engage in online networking to connect with others in your field.

2. Contribute to Your Community Active participation is key to building a vibrant and supportive community. By contributing your time, skills, and resources, you help create a stronger, more connected environment.

Volunteer Your Time: Volunteering is a powerful way to give back to your community. Whether it's helping out at a local charity, mentoring others, or organizing events, your contributions make a meaningful impact.

Share Your Skills and Knowledge: Everyone has something valuable to offer. Sharing your skills, expertise, or knowledge with others—whether through teaching, mentoring, or simply offering advice—enriches the community and strengthens bonds.

Support Others: Show up for others in your community by attending their events, celebrating their successes, and offering help when needed. Your support reinforces the sense of connection and belonging.

3. Foster Inclusivity and Diversity A thriving community is one that embraces diversity and inclusivity, where everyone feels welcome and valued. Fostering an inclusive environment enhances the richness and resilience of the community.

Embrace Differences: Celebrate the diversity of your community by engaging with people from different backgrounds, cultures, and perspectives. Learn from their experiences and appreciate the unique contributions they bring.

Encourage Participation: Ensure that everyone in your community has the opportunity to participate and contribute. Create spaces where all voices are heard and respected, and actively seek out input from those who may feel marginalized.

Promote Equity: Advocate for fair treatment and equal opportunities within your community. Address issues of inequality and work towards creating an environment where everyone can thrive.

4. Build a Sense of Belonging A strong community is one where members feel a deep sense of belonging and connection. Creating opportunities for interaction, collaboration, and celebration helps foster this sense of belonging.

Organize Community Events: Events such as block parties, cultural festivals, or group outings provide opportunities for people to connect and build relationships. These gatherings help create shared experiences and memories.

Create Shared Spaces: Physical spaces, such as community centers, parks, or coworking spaces, serve as hubs for interaction and collaboration. These spaces encourage people to come together and engage in meaningful ways.

Celebrate Together: Recognize and celebrate the milestones, achievements, and cultural traditions of your community members. Celebrations reinforce a sense of unity and shared identity.

The Role of Digital Communities

In today's digital age, online communities have become an increasingly important part of our social landscape. While they differ from traditional face-to-face communities, digital communities offer unique opportunities for connection, learning, and support.

1. The Benefits of Digital Communities

Accessibility: Online communities are accessible to people regardless of location, time zone, or mobility. They allow you to connect with others who share your interests, even if they live on the other side of the world.

Diverse Perspectives: Digital communities bring together people from diverse backgrounds, providing exposure to different cultures, ideas, and viewpoints. This diversity enriches the conversation and broadens your understanding.

Ongoing Engagement: Unlike traditional communities that may meet sporadically, digital communities offer continuous engagement. Social media, forums, and group chats provide spaces for ongoing interaction and support.

2. Building and Participating in Online Communities Engaging in online communities requires a different approach than face-to-face interactions. Building meaningful connections in a digital space involves intentionality, respect, and active participation.

Choose Your Platforms Wisely: Select online communities that align with your interests and values. Whether it's a social media group, a professional network, or a discussion forum, ensure the community fosters positive, respectful interactions.

Contribute Positively: Be an active participant in the community by contributing valuable content, offering support, and engaging in discussions. Avoid negativity, trolling, or divisive behavior, which can harm the community's atmosphere.

Maintain Boundaries: While digital communities can be a great source of support, it's important to maintain boundaries. Balance your online interactions with offline activities, and be mindful of the time you spend in digital spaces.

3. Blending Online and Offline Communities While online communities offer many benefits, they shouldn't replace face-to-face interactions. Instead, look for ways to blend your digital and offline connections for a more balanced and fulfilling social life.

Meet in Person: Whenever possible, take online connections offline by meeting in person. Whether it's attending a conference, organizing a local meetup, or simply having coffee with a fellow community member, face-to-face interactions deepen your connection.

Hybrid Communities: Many communities now offer hybrid models, combining online and offline activities. These might include virtual meetings, webinars, or online forums paired with in-person events and gatherings.

Use Technology to Enhance Offline Connections: Technology can also enhance your offline relationships. Use messaging apps, video calls, or social media to stay in touch with friends and family, especially when distance makes in-person meetings difficult.

Overcoming Barriers to Connection

While the benefits of community and connection are clear, many people face barriers that make it difficult to build and maintain relationships. Whether due to social anxiety, past experiences, or simply a busy lifestyle, these barriers can be challenging to overcome.

1. Social Anxiety and Shyness Social anxiety and shyness can make it difficult to engage with others, leading to feelings of isolation and loneliness. However, with practice and support, it's possible to overcome these challenges and build meaningful connections.

Start Small: Begin by engaging in low-pressure social situations, such as attending a small gathering or joining a casual group activity. Gradually increase your social interactions as you become more comfortable.

Focus on Others: Shifting your focus from yourself to others can help reduce anxiety. Instead of worrying about how you're perceived, concentrate on getting to know the other person and showing genuine interest in them.

Seek Support: If social anxiety is significantly impacting your ability to connect with others, consider seeking support from a therapist or counselor. Cognitive-behavioral therapy (CBT) and other therapeutic approaches can be highly effective in managing social anxiety.

2. Past Negative Experiences Past negative experiences, such as betrayal, rejection, or loss, can create fear and hesitation around forming new connections. However, it's important to remember that not all relationships will mirror past experiences.

Acknowledge Your Feelings: It's natural to feel apprehensive after a negative experience. Acknowledge your feelings and give yourself time to heal, but don't let past hurts prevent you from forming new relationships.

Take Things Slowly: When building new relationships, take things slowly. Allow trust to develop gradually, and don't rush into deep connections before you're ready.

Focus on Positive Relationships: Surround yourself with positive, supportive people who uplift and encourage you. These relationships can help rebuild your confidence in connecting with others.

3. Busy Lifestyles In today's fast-paced world, it can be challenging to find time for meaningful connections. However, prioritizing relationships is crucial for your well-being and personal growth.

Schedule Social Time: Just as you would schedule work or exercise, schedule time for social interactions. Whether it's a weekly coffee with a friend or a monthly family dinner, making time for connections helps maintain relationships.

Integrate Socializing into Your Routine: Look for opportunities to connect with others within your existing routine. For example, invite a colleague for a walk during your lunch break, or attend a fitness class with a friend.

Simplify and Prioritize: If your schedule is overwhelming, consider simplifying and prioritizing. Focus on the most meaningful relationships and activities, and let go of commitments that don't align with your values.

Conclusion: The Lifelong Value of Community and Connection

Community and connection are the threads that weave the fabric of our lives. They provide us with support, belonging, and purpose, enriching our experiences and helping us grow. By actively cultivating strong, meaningful relationships and contributing to the communities we are part of, we create a network of support that sustains us through life's challenges and joys.

As you continue on your journey of personal growth, remember that you are not alone. The people around you—family, friends, colleagues, neighbors, and even strangers—are all part of your extended community. Embrace the opportunities to connect, support, and be supported, knowing that these relationships are among the most valuable resources you have.

Whether through a smile, a helping hand, or a shared experience, every connection you make has the potential to impact your life and the lives of others in profound ways. Cherish these connections, invest in them, and allow them to be a source of strength, inspiration, and joy as you navigate the journey of life.

CHAPTER TWENTY-TWO

MOVING FORWARD

Moving Forward: A Roadmap for Continued Growth

Introduction: Growth as a Lifelong Journey

Personal growth is not a one-time achievement; it is an ongoing journey. Each step forward offers new lessons, challenges, and opportunities for self-discovery and improvement. The concept of "growth" isn't about reaching a final destination but embracing a continuous process of learning, evolving, and becoming a better version of yourself.

In this chapter, we'll explore practical steps for maintaining personal growth over time. You will learn how to set new goals, remain adaptable in the face of change, and cultivate habits that ensure long-term success. Whether you're at the beginning of your journey or already well on your way, this roadmap will provide you with the tools and insights needed to keep moving forward with purpose and resilience.

1. Reflecting on Where You Are Now

Before charting a path forward, it's essential to reflect on where you currently stand in your personal growth journey. Reflection helps you evaluate the progress you've made, the lessons you've learned, and the areas where you still have room to grow.

Steps for Reflective Evaluation:

Review Your Past Goals: Look back at the goals you've previously set. Which ones did you achieve, and which ones remain unfulfilled? What challenges did you encounter along the way, and how did you overcome them?

Identify Key Learnings: Consider the lessons you've learned from both successes and failures. How have these experiences shaped your mindset, values, and behaviors? What new skills or strengths have you developed?

Assess Your Current State: Where do you feel most fulfilled, and where do you feel lacking? Identify areas of your life—such as career, relationships, health, or personal development—that you want to focus on moving forward.

Reflection Exercise:

Take 30 minutes to journal about your personal growth journey so far. Write about the biggest challenges you've faced, the milestones you've achieved, and how you've changed. This reflection will serve as the foundation for setting future goals.

2. Setting New Goals for Continued Growth

Goal setting is an essential part of personal growth, helping you stay focused and motivated. As you move forward, it's important to set new goals that reflect your current aspirations and challenges. However, these goals should evolve with you, adapting to your changing circumstances and desires.

SMART Goals Framework (Revisited):

Specific: Your new goals should be clear and well-defined.

Measurable: Ensure that you can track your progress and measure success.

Achievable: Set realistic goals that challenge you but remain attainable.

Relevant: Align your goals with your values and long-term vision.

Time-bound: Set deadlines for achieving your goals, but remain flexible as life evolves.

Types of Goals to Consider:

Personal Growth Goals: Focus on developing new skills, building emotional intelligence, or enhancing your mental and physical well-being.

Example: "Practice mindfulness meditation for 15 minutes every day for the next three months."

Professional Growth Goals: Set goals related to career advancement, skill acquisition, or expanding your professional network.

Example: "Complete an online certification in digital marketing by the end of the year."

Relationship Goals: Improve the quality of your relationships, whether with family, friends, or colleagues.

Example: "Spend one weekend each month reconnecting with close friends through shared activities."

Goal-Setting Exercise:

Write down five new goals that align with your current stage of life. For each goal, include specific action steps, deadlines, and potential obstacles you may face.

3. Developing Consistent Habits for Long-Term Success

Achieving sustained growth requires more than just setting goals—it requires developing daily habits that support your aspirations. Habits are the small, consistent actions that compound over time, leading to significant progress.

The Power of Habit Formation:

Start Small: Focus on creating simple, manageable habits that are easy to integrate into your daily routine. Small habits are easier to stick to and gradually build momentum.

Example: Instead of committing to an hour of exercise every day, start with 10 minutes of movement.

Be Consistent: Consistency is key to turning actions into habits. Make a commitment to show up for yourself every day, even if progress feels slow.

Track Your Progress: Use a habit tracker or journal to monitor your progress. Visualizing your consistency can motivate you to keep going.

Habit Creation Framework:

Cue: Identify a specific trigger that prompts the habit (e.g., waking up triggers your meditation practice).

Routine: Perform the habit immediately after the cue (e.g., meditating right after waking up).

Reward: Reinforce the habit by rewarding yourself after completing the action (e.g., enjoy a cup of tea after your meditation session).

Building Keystone Habits: Keystone habits are the foundational habits that have a ripple effect on other areas of your life. By focusing on developing just one or two keystone habits, you can create positive changes across the board.

Examples of Keystone Habits:

Exercise: Regular physical activity can improve your energy levels, boost your mood, and enhance your productivity.

Healthy Eating: Maintaining a balanced diet can lead to better physical health, mental clarity, and emotional stability.

Journaling: Writing regularly can help you process your thoughts, set clearer goals, and track your personal growth.

Habit-Building Exercise:

Identify one keystone habit that you want to develop over the next month. Break it down into a manageable routine and use the habit creation framework to integrate it into your daily life.

4. Embracing Change and Adaptability

One of the greatest challenges to continued growth is learning to adapt to change. Life is unpredictable, and circumstances can shift unexpectedly. Cultivating adaptability allows you to maintain your growth trajectory, even when the path forward isn't clear.

Strategies for Embracing Change:

Maintain a Growth Mindset: View change as an opportunity to learn and grow rather than something to fear. A growth mindset helps you stay resilient in the face of uncertainty.

Example: Instead of resisting a job transition, see it as an opportunity to develop new skills or explore a different career path.

Practice Flexibility: Be willing to adjust your goals and plans as circumstances evolve. Flexibility allows you to pivot when necessary without feeling like you've failed.

Example: If your plan to exercise five days a week becomes unsustainable, adjust it to three days and continue making progress.

Seek Opportunities in Challenges: Every challenge presents an opportunity for growth. When faced with difficulties, ask yourself, "What can I learn from this experience?"

Dealing with Setbacks:

Reframe Setbacks: Instead of seeing setbacks as failures, view them as learning experiences. Reflect on what went wrong and how you can use the experience to improve.

Keep Moving Forward: Setbacks are a natural part of growth, but they don't define your journey. Stay focused on your long-term vision and take small steps forward, even when progress feels slow.

Adaptability Exercise:

Think of a recent change or challenge you've faced. Write down how you initially responded and then list three ways you can reframe the situation to focus on the positive opportunities for growth.

5. Maintaining a Support System

Growth is often seen as a personal journey, but it is equally important to acknowledge the role that others play in our development. A strong support system—composed of family, friends, mentors, or colleagues—can provide encouragement, guidance, and accountability.

Building Your Support Network:

Identify Key Relationships: Consider the people in your life who offer support, whether emotional, professional, or practical. These individuals will be crucial in helping you stay on track with your goals.

Seek Out Mentors: Mentorship can be invaluable for personal and professional growth. A mentor offers experience, insight, and constructive feedback, helping you navigate challenges and make informed decisions.

Example: If you're pursuing a new career path, find someone who has already succeeded in that field and seek their guidance.

Join a Community: Surrounding yourself with like-minded individuals fosters a sense of belonging and shared purpose. Whether it's a local group or an online community, finding people who are also committed to personal growth will help keep you motivated.

Nurturing Your Support System:

Give and Receive Support: A healthy support system is based on mutual respect and reciprocity. Be there for others in your network when they need help, and don't hesitate to ask for support when you need it.

Communicate Regularly: Maintain open lines of communication with the key people in your life. Regular check-ins, whether through phone calls, texts, or in-person meetings, help strengthen your connections.

Celebrate Wins Together: Share your successes with your support system, and celebrate their achievements as well. Celebrating together fosters a sense of shared accomplishment.

Support System Exercise:

Make a list of the five most supportive people in your life. Reflect on how each individual has contributed to your growth, and consider ways you can continue to nurture those relationships.

6. The Importance of Reflection and Rest

While striving for continued growth, it's easy to fall into the trap of constant productivity. However, reflection and rest are critical components of sustainable growth. Taking time to rest allows you to recharge, while regular reflection helps you assess your progress and realign your goals.

The Role of Rest in Growth:

Avoiding Burnout: Pushing yourself too hard without rest can lead to burnout, which ultimately hinders your progress. Incorporate regular breaks and downtime into your routine to maintain balance.

Enhancing Creativity and Problem-Solving: Rest allows your mind to wander, often leading to creative breakthroughs and new perspectives. Whether through sleep, meditation, or relaxation, rest supports your cognitive and emotional well-being.

Reflection as a Tool for Growth:

Regular Self-Check-ins: Schedule regular check-ins with yourself—weekly, monthly, or quarterly—where you reflect on your goals, habits, and overall well-being. Use these moments to celebrate progress, address challenges, and adjust your approach.

Journaling: Journaling is a powerful tool for reflection. Writing about your experiences, emotions, and insights helps you process your thoughts and track your growth over time.

Rest and Reflection Exercise:

Dedicate one day a week to rest and reflection. Use this time to disconnect from work, engage in relaxing activities, and journal about your personal growth.

7. Staying Committed to Lifelong Learning

Personal growth requires a commitment to lifelong learning. Staying curious, open-minded, and eager to expand your knowledge ensures that you continue evolving.

Ways to Embrace Lifelong Learning:

Read Regularly: Make reading a habit, whether it's books, articles, or blogs related to your interests. Reading exposes you to new ideas, perspectives, and knowledge.

Take Courses or Workshops: Continuing education, whether formal or informal, keeps your mind sharp and helps you develop new skills. Explore online courses, attend workshops, or join webinars on topics that interest you.

Learn from Others: Conversations with others—whether friends, mentors, or even strangers—can provide valuable insights. Be open to learning from those around you, and seek out diverse viewpoints.

Cultivating Curiosity:

Ask Questions: Stay curious by asking questions about the world around you. Embrace a mindset of curiosity in your personal and professional life, and explore new areas of interest.

Experiment and Explore: Don't be afraid to try new things, even if they seem outside your comfort zone. Whether it's picking up a new hobby, exploring a different career path, or traveling to unfamiliar places, exploring new experiences fuels growth.

Lifelong Learning Exercise:

Identify one new skill or subject you want to explore over the next six months. Create a plan for how you'll learn—whether through reading, taking a course, or practicing—and set aside dedicated time each week to focus on this area.

8. Celebrating Your Progress and Achievements

As you move forward, it's important to take time to celebrate your progress and achievements. Recognizing your accomplishments—whether big or small—reinforces positive behaviors and motivates you to continue growing.

Celebration Strategies:

Acknowledge Milestones: Break your larger goals into smaller milestones, and celebrate when you reach each one. This could be as simple as treating yourself to a favorite activity or sharing your success with friends.

Reflect on Growth: Look back at where you started and how far you've come. Reflect on the challenges you've overcome and the lessons you've learned. Recognizing your growth helps you stay motivated and inspired.

Reward Yourself: Give yourself rewards for achieving your goals, whether it's a day off, a special purchase, or a trip you've been wanting to take. These rewards reinforce your hard work and remind you of the importance of balance in the growth process.

Celebration Exercise:

List three recent achievements or milestones in your personal growth journey. Write down how you will celebrate each one, and take time to acknowledge the hard work that went into reaching these goals.

Conclusion: Embrace the Journey Ahead

Personal growth is not a linear path but a dynamic and evolving journey. As you move forward, remember that growth requires patience, adaptability, and resilience. The roadmap outlined in this chapter provides you with practical strategies to continue growing, but the true power of growth lies in your commitment to lifelong learning and self-discovery.

Each step you take brings you closer to the person you are meant to become. Embrace the challenges, celebrate the successes, and stay open to the opportunities that arise along the way. As you continue on your journey, know that every decision you make, every habit you form, and every lesson you learn contributes to your ongoing evolution.

The journey of growth is lifelong, and while the path may twist and turn, you have the tools, mindset, and support system to navigate it with confidence. Stay committed to your goals, be kind to yourself through setbacks, and always keep moving forward.

Dear Readers

As we conclude this journey through a world that often seems hopeless, I want to leave you with a final thought. The stories and reflections within these pages are a testament to the enduring strength of the human spirit. In a world where darkness may seem overwhelming, remember that hope is not a passive wish but an active force—a choice to believe in the possibility of a better tomorrow.

May these pages inspire you to find light in your own life, to seek out moments of resilience and courage, and to spread hope wherever you go. For it is through our collective acts of hope and kindness that we create the change we wish to see in the world.

Thank you for joining me on this journey. Keep believing, keep striving, and keep hoping.

With heartfelt gratitude,

Ashfaq Ahmed

Feel free to ask it to better fit your tone and message!

E-mail: ashfaqmotivation337@gmail.com

Special Thanks

AMITA SONI

I would like to extend my deepest gratitude to my dearest friend, **Amita Soni.** Your unwavering support, insightful feedback, and boundless encouragement have been instrumental in bringing this book to life.

In the countless hours we spent discussing ideas, brainstorming solutions, and navigating through the challenging moments of this journey, your presence was a constant source of inspiration and strength. Your belief in this project, even during its most uncertain times, has been a beacon of hope and a reminder of the power of true friendship.

Amita, your generosity and dedication have touched my heart deeply. Thank you for standing by me, for being a guiding light, and for sharing in the dream of this book. Your contribution goes far beyond mere assistance; it has been a profound part of the creative process and the emotional essence of this work.

To my cherished friend, Amita Soni.

Words cannot fully convey the depth of my gratitude for your incredible support throughout this journey. Your unwavering faith, insightful guidance, and boundless encouragement have been more than just assistance—they have been a source of inspiration and a cornerstone of my strength.

From the first spark of an idea to the final touches of this book, your presence has been a constant, comforting force. Your belief in this project, even when I faltered, and your commitment to helping it come to fruition, have been nothing short of extraordinary. In each moment of doubt and every challenge faced, you were there with a steady hand and a compassionate heart.

Amita, your contribution has woven a thread of hope and perseverance into every page of this book. Your wisdom and kindness have illuminated the path forward, and your friendship has been a gift I deeply treasure.

As you move forward in your own journey, I wish for you a future as bright and fulfilling as the light you have brought into my life. May you find success, joy, and boundless opportunities, and may your own dreams unfold with the same grace and beauty that you have shared with me.

Thank you for being not only a friend but a true partner in this endeavor. Your spirit and support have made all the difference, and for that, I am forever grateful.

With profound appreciation and heartfelt wishes,
Ashfaq Ahmed

Special Thanks

BALWANT SINGH SIR

To my esteemed teacher, **Balwant Singh sir.**

With deepest respect and gratitude, I dedicate this special thanks to you. Your inspiration and guidance have been the driving forces behind the creation of this book. Your belief in the power of words and the importance of storytelling has profoundly impacted me, sparking the passion and commitment that shaped this work.

Your wisdom, encouragement, and insightful critique have been invaluable throughout this journey. From the very beginning, you saw potential where I saw only uncertainty, and your unwavering support has been a beacon of motivation and clarity.

Balwant Singh sir, your dedication to nurturing my growth as a writer has made an indelible mark on this book and on my heart. Your influence extends far beyond the confines of the classroom; it has inspired me to pursue my dreams with confidence and to express my deepest thoughts and emotions through this work.

As I move forward, I carry with me the lessons you've imparted and the inspiration you've provided. I am profoundly grateful for your mentorship and for the role you've played in this creative journey.

May your own path be filled with continued success and fulfillment, and may you continue to inspire and guide others as you have so generously done for me.

With sincere appreciation and admiration,

Your lovely student

Ashfaq Ahmed

www.ingramcontent.com/pod-product-compliance
Lightning Source LLC
Chambersburg PA
CBHW070903160726
48004CB00003B/1219